hampstead theatre

HAMPSTEAD THEATRE AND THE PETER WOLFF THEATRE TRUST
PRESENT THE WORLD PREMIERE OF

US and Them
by Tamsin Oglesby

Cast (in alphabetical order)

Martin Phillips **Hugh Bonneville**
Waiter / Maynard / Timothy **Paul Courtenay Hyu**
Jay Marshall **Jonah Y Lotan**
Ed Marshall **Matthew Marsh**
Charlotte Gardner **Siobhan Redmond**
Izzie Gardner **Jemima Rooper**
Lori Marshall **Harriet Walter**

Director **Jennie Darnell**
Designer **Matthew Wright**
Lighting **Jason Taylor**
Sound **Scott George** for **Aura**
Composer **Joby Talbot**

Costume Supervisor **Anna Barcock**
Assistant Stage Manager **Emma Barrow**
Casting Director **Carol Dudley**, CDG, CSA
Projection System Designer **Scott George** for **Aura**
Chief Electrician **Greg Gould**
Deputy Chief Electrician **Chris Harris**
Company Stage Manager **Julie Issott**
Assistant Director **Henry Mason**
Deputy Stage Manager **Charlotte Padgham**
Production Manager **John Titcombe**
Stage Manager **Sarah Tryfan**
Technical Manager **David Tuff**
Assistant Electrician **Simon Williams**
Wardrobe Maintenance **Selina Wong**

Press Representative **Charlotte Eilenberg**
charlotte.eilenberg@dsl.pipex.com

US and Them had its opening night at
Hampstead Theatre on 28 May 2003.

A Hampstead Theatre commission.

Incidental music by Joby Talbot by
arrangement with Chester Music Limited.

thank you

John Clive / Andy Edwards
Stephen Jones / Adam Woodward

The Company

Tamsin Oglesby Writer

Tamsin's first play **Two Lips Indifferent Red** was produced at the Bush Theatre in 1995. It was nominated for the Susan Smith Blackburn award and optioned as a screenplay. Her second play, **My Best Friend**, was commissioned by Birmingham Repertory Theatre and opened at Hampstead Theatre in January 2000 before moving to Birmingham Repertory Theatre. Her third play, **Olive**, was commissioned by the National Theatre for International Connections. It was performed there and all around the country.

Previously Tamsin worked as a director at the Royal Court, National Studio and on the London Fringe.

Hugh Bonneville Martin Phillips

Theatre includes: **The Handyman** (Chichester Festival Theatre); **Habeas Corpus** (Donmar Warehouse); **My Night With Reg** (Criterion); **The Devil's Disciple, School for Scandal, Juno and the Paycock, Entertaining Strangers, Yerma, School for Wives** (National Theatre); **Beautiful Thing** (Bush Theatre tour / Donmar Warehouse); **Hamlet, Amphibians, The Alchemist, 'Tis Pity She's a Whore, Two Gentlemen of Verona, The Virtuoso** (Royal Shakespeare Company) and seasons at the Colchester Mercury, Leicester Haymarket and The Open Air Theatre, Regent's Park.

Television includes: **Wren, Impact, Philip Larkin: Love Again, The Commander, Daniel Deronda, Dr Zhivago, Tipping the Velvet, The Gathering Storm, Hans Christian Andersen, Midsomer Murders, Armadillo, The Cazalets, Take a Girl Like You, Thursday 12th, Madame Bovary, Murder Most Horrid, Holding the Baby, The Scold's Bridle, Heat of the Sun, Mosley, Get Well Soon, See You Friday, Breakout, Married For Life, Bugs, The Man Who Made Husbands Jealous, Punt and Dennis, The Vet, Stick With Me Kid, Between the Lines, Peak Practice, Sherlock Holmes, Cadfael** and **Stalagluft.**

Films include: **Conspiracy of Silence, Iris, The Emperor's New Clothes, High Heels and Low Lifes, Blow Dry, Mansfield Park, Notting Hill, Tomorrow Never Dies** and **Frankenstein.**

Paul Courtenay Hyu
Waiter / Maynard / Timothy

Theatre includes: **Martha, Josie and the Chinese Elvis** (Watford Palace / Bolton Octagon / Liverpool Everyman); **Wheel of Life** (Gielgud Theatre); **Hiawatha** (Royal Lyceum Theatre); **The Merchant of Venice** (Cardiff Sherman); **Cinderella** (Arts Theatre); **The Wind in the Willows** (National Theatre at the Old Vic); **Takeaway** (Lyric Hammersmith); **Miss Saigon** (Theatre Royal) and **Three Japanese Women** (Soho Theatre).

Television includes: **Casualty, Manchild, The Bill, Clocking Off, Eastenders, Dr**

Terrible's House of Horrible, North Square and **Trial and Retribution V.**

Film includes: **The Lost Battalion, Wing Commander** and **The First 9½ Weeks.**

Radio includes: **Hitler's Buddha, A Many Splendoured Thing, Black Walls, Fifteen-Love, Devils in the Glass** and **The Adventures of Tin Tin.**

Matthew Marsh Ed Marshall

Theatre includes: **The Day You'll Love Me** (Hampstead Theatre); **The Lodger** (Hampstead Theatre / Royal Exchange Manchester); **A Buyer's Market** (Bush Theatre); **The Little Foxes** (Donmar Warehouse); **Conversations After a Burial** (Almeida Theatre / tour); **Copenhagen** (National Theatre / West End); **Broken Glass** (National Theatre tour); **Resistance** (Old Red Lion); **The Last Yankee** (Duke of Yorks Theatre); **All My Sons, Comedians, Measure for Measure, Who's Afraid of Virginia Woolf?, Julius Caesar, The Crucible, Hamlet, Stags and Hens, The Jail Diary of Albie Sachs** (Young Vic) and **Marya** (Old Vic).

Television includes: **Wall of Silence, The Commander, Midsomer Murders, Real Men, Murder in Mind, Silent Witness, The Cazalet Chronicles, Lock Stock, Big**

Bad World, New Born, A Certain Justice, Getting Hurt, Heartbeat, A Respectable Trade, Into the Blue, Game On, Death of a Salesman, Madson, The Turnaround, Into the Fire, Crocodile Shoes, A Touch of Frost, Gengis Cohn, Between the Lines, Speaker of Mandarin, Sam Saturday, Red Dwarf V, Chancer, A Taste for Death, An Affair in Mind and **The Monocled Mutineer.**

Film includes: **Blackball, Bad Company, Miranda, Spy Game, Jimmy Fizz, Quicksand, Smilla's Sense of Snow, Alambrado, Dirty Weekend, Mountains of the Moon, Diamond Skulls** and **The Fourth Protocol.**

Jonah Y Lotan Jay Marshall

Jonah trained at LAMDA.

Theatre includes: **This Is Our Youth**
(Garrick Theatre) and **All's Well That Ends
Well, Coriolanus, Ivanov, The White Devil**
(LAMDA).

Television includes: **Joyce, The Brown**

Sisters and **Relic
Hunter.**

Film includes:
**Swimming Pool,
Lost Change** and
Domino.

Siobhan Redmond Charlotte Gardner

Siobhan trained at Bristol Old Vic
Theatre School.

Theatre includes: **Perfect Days**
(Hampstead Theatre / West End / tour /
Traverse Theatre); **The Prime of Miss Jean
Brodie, As You Like It** (Lyceum,
Edinburgh); **Les Liaisons Dangereuses**
(PW Productions); **Spanish Tragedy, Much
Ado About Nothing** (Royal Shakespeare
Company); **An Experienced Woman Gives
Advice** (Manchester Royal Exchange); **The
Trick is to Keep Breathing** (Tron Theatre,
Glasgow / Toronto / Royal Court);
**A Midsummer Night's Dream, King Lear,
Look Back in Anger** (Renaissance Theatre
Company); **Carmen** (Communicado
Theatre Company); **Shadowing the
Conqueror** (Traverse Theatre / Edinburgh
Festival); **The Big Picture** (Dundee Rep);
Goldilocks (Grand Opera House, Belfast);
A Month of Sundays (Nuffield Theatre /
Duchess Theatre); **Macbeth** (Tron Theatre,
Glasgow) and **Don Juan the Lover**
(Sheffield Crucible).

Television includes:
**Holby City, Every
Woman Knows a
Secret, In The Red,
Wokenwell,
Throwaways,
Deacon Brodie,
Nervous Energy,
Relative Stranger, Sorry About Last Night,
The High Life, Rab C Nesbitt, Between
the Lines, Dad on Arrival, Rides, At the
End of Alex Cording, Gravy Train, Look
Back in Anger, Hard Cases, The
Dunroman Rising, Tea Bags, Bulman,
Taggart, Sweet Nothings, Alfresco** and
Nothing to Worry About.

Film includes: **Beautiful People, Karmic
Mothers, Captives** and **Latin for a Dark
Room.**

Radio includes: **The Trick is to Keep
Breathing, Beaumarchais, Mary Queen of
Scots Got Her Head Chopped Off,
McLevy, The House, Maleficium** and **Miss
Smilla's Feeling for Snow.**

Jemima Rooper Izzie Gardner

Theatre includes: **Where Do We Live, Rampage, Worker's Writes** (Royal Court) and **Oscar** (The King's Head).

Television includes: three series of **As If** for Channel 4, **Love in a Cold Climate, Urban Gothic, The Railway Children, Dance, Lifeforce, Summer in the Suburbs, Wives and Daughter, The Passion, Junk, Animal Ark** and **The Famous Five.**

Film includes: **A Sound of Thunder, Snapshots, Owd Bob, Willy's War** and **The Higher Mortals.**

Harriet Walter Lori Marshall

Theatre includes: **Sweet Panic. La Musica** (Hampstead Theatre); **Dinner, Life X 3, Children's Hour, Arcadia** (National Theatre) and **The Royal Family** (Theatre Royal Haymarket). For the Royal Shakespeare Company: **Much Ado About Nothing** (also Haymarket), **Macbeth, The Duchess of Malfi, Cymbeline, Twelfth Night, A Question of Geography, Three Sisters, The Castle, All's Well That Ends Well, The Twin Rivals, Henry IV** (Parts I & II), **The Witch of Edmonton** and **Nicholas Nickelby.** For the Royal Court: **Three Birds Alighting on a Field** (also Manhattan Theatre Club), **The Lucky Chance, The Seagull** (Irish version), **Cloud Nine, Three More Sleepless Nights** and **Hamlet.** Other theatre: **The Late Middle Classes** (Palace Theatre Watford); **Ivanov** (Almeida Theatre); **Hedda Gabler** (Chichester Festival Theatre); **Old Times** (Wyndhams), **The Merchant of Venice** (Royal Exchange Manchester); **Three Sisters** (Theatre Royal, Bristol); **The Possessed** (Paris / Milan / Bologna / Ameida Theatre) and **The Ragged Trousered Philanthropist** (Joint Stock / Riverside Studios).

Television includes: **Peter Ackroyd's London, George Eliot: A Scandalous Life, My Uncle Silas, Waking the Dead, Macbeth, Leprechauns, Normal Ormal, Unfinished Business, A Dance to the Music of Time, Inspector Morse, Ashenden, The Men's Room, They Never Slept, Benefactors, Dorothy L. Sayers, Mysteries, The Price, The Cherry Orchard** and **The Imitation Game.** French TV: **La Nuit Miraculeuse.**

Film includes: **Bright Young Things, Villa Des Roses, Onegin, Bedrooms & Hallways, Keep the Aspidistra Flying, The Governess, The Leading Man, Sense and Sensibility, The Hour of the Pig, Milou en Mai, The Good Father, Turtle Diary** and **Reflections.**

Books: **Other People's Shoes** (to be re-issued by Nick Hern Books September 2003) and **Macbeth** for Faber's 'Actors on Shakespeare' series.

Jennie Darnell Director

Jennie Darnell studied at the Universities of London and Sheffield where she gained her Master of Arts degree in Theatre and Film.

Jennie is Associate Director at Hampstead Theatre for whom she directed **The Dead Eye Boy**. She was previously an Associate Director for Plymouth Theatre Royal. Her productions at Plymouth included the UK premiere of Wedekind's **Musik, The Impostor** (a contemporary spin on Moliere's **Tartuffe**), **Blood Red, Saffron Yellow, Union Street, True West** (co-production with Salisbury Playhouse), **All My Sons, Burn This** and **The Woman Who Cooked Her Husband**. She was also an Associate Director for **Art** at The Whitehall and Wyndhams Theatres and directed **Life X 3** on tour and at The Savoy.

In 1993 Jennie won a place on the Regional Theatre Young Directors' Scheme to work at Nottingham Playhouse where her productions included **Rumpelstiltskin, Pandora, Telling Tales** and **The Woman Who Cooked Her Husband**. In 1996 she received an Arts Council Bursary to be a Resident Associate Director at West Yorkshire Playhouse where she directed **Office Suite** and **The Messiah**.

Other directing credits include: **Telephone Belles, Traffic Hearts** (The Steam Factory); **Lady Windermere's Fan** (Salisbury Playhouse); **Up on the Roof** (Mercury Theatre, Colchester); **Wallflowering** (national tour); **Deja Vu** (Croydon International Playwriting Festival) and **Marat / Sade** (Central School of Speech and Drama).

Matthew Wright Designer

Matthew designed **The Dead Eye Boy** at Hampstead Theatre.

Recent credits include: **The Green Man** (Bush Theatre / Theatre Royal Plymouth); **Larkin with Women** (West Yorkshire Playhouse); **Getting to the Foot of the Mountain** (Birmingham Rep); and **Arcadia, Amy's View** (Salisbury Playhouse / Theatre Royal Northampton).

Other credits include: **Royal Supreme, Blood Red, Saffron Yellow, Musik, The Imposter** (Theatre Royal Plymouth); **The Deep Blue Sea, A Taste of Honey** (Watford Palace); **Romeo and Juliet** (Greenwich Theatre / tour); **The End of the Affair** (Bridewell Theatre / Salisbury Playhouse); **Twelfth Night, Hamlet** (Oxford Stage Company); **Swamp City** (Birmingham Rep); **Pow!** (Paines Plough) and **Hamlet** (National Theatre, staged in Brixton Prison).

Opera includes: **Il Pomo D'Oro** (Batignano Opera Festival); **Don Pasquale** (Scottish Opera Go Round).

Matthew also designed the costumes for **Seriously Funny** on Channel 4.

Jason Taylor Lighting

Current and recent work includes: **The Dead Eye Boy** (Hampstead Theatre); **Hobson's Choice, Yerma** (Manchester Royal Exchange); **Abigail's Party** (New Ambassadors Theatre / Whitehall Theatre); **Little Shop of Horrors** (West Yorkshire Playhouse); **My Night with Reg / Dealers Choice** (Birmingham Rep); **The Clearing** (Shared Experience); **Single Spies** (national tour); **Sitting Pretty** (national tour); **Pirates of Penzance** (national tour); **Office** (Edinburgh International Festival); **Hedda Gabler, Snake in Fridge** (Manchester Royal Exchange); **Iolanthe, The Mikado, Yeoman of the Guard** (Savoy Theatre) and last year's Labour Party Conference.

Jason has lit over 150 other productions including: 14 seasons at the Open Air Theatre, **Kindertransport** (Vaudeville Theatre); **Rosencrantz and Guildenstern** (Piccadilly Theatre); **And Then There Were None** (Duke of York's Theatre) and **Great Balls of Fire** (Cambridge Theatre). Other London work includes productions at the Bush Theatre, Bridewell Theatre and numerous productions for Soho Theatre. Jason has also designed at most major regional theatres including Nottingham, Sheffield, Plymouth, West Yorkshire Playhouse, Birmingham, Edinburgh, Scarborough, Southampton, Clwyd and Liverpool. Jason was also lighting consultant for the new Soho Theatre, London and the Open Air Theatre, Regents Park.

Scott George for Aura Sound

Recent sound design credits include: **Fragile Land, The Safari Party** (Hampstead Theatre); **Midnight's Children** (Royal Shakespeare Company); **Cabaret** (Chichester Festival Theatre); **Kosher Harry** (Royal Court); **Sive** (Druid Theatre Company, Ireland); **Maria Friedman In Concert** (West End); **Taming of the Shrew** (Nottingham Playhouse); **The Witches, Bali, Death of a Salesman, Dolly West's Kitchen, Peter Pan** (Haymarket Theatre, Leicester); **Naked Talent Season** (Bush Theatre); **The Lost Musicals** (Royal Opera House); **Much Ado About Nothing** (London International Festival at The Guildhall) and **The Three Musketeers** (Young Vic). Production engineering

credits include: **International Festival of Musical Theatre** (Cardiff); **Benefactors** (tour and West End); **Distance from Here** (Almeida Theatre); **Macbeth** (Ludlow Festival); **Saturday Night Fever** (British tour); **Lulu, Coriolanus / Richard II** (Almeida Theatre at Gainsborough Studios, New York and Tokyo); **Macbeth** (Royal Shakespeare Company tour) and **Plenty** (Almeida Theatre at The Albery).

In July 2000, Scott became Show-Control Director of Aura Sound Design Ltd. a London based design company founded in January 1998. The company's work has since been heard across UK, Europe, USA, Canada and the Far East.

Joby Talbot Composer

Joby began writing and performing in 1993. His classical music, television scores and pop collaborations are performed and broadcast all over the world.

Joby's early television scores for the BBC include the theme music for **Young Musician of the Year, Tomorrow's World** (co-written with Neil Hannon) and the score for **Queen's Park Story** (BBC 2). He later composed scores for two major series of **Chambers** (BBC Entertainment) and **The League of Gentlemen** (Best Title Music award in 2000, Royal Television Society).

In 2000, the British Film Institute commissioned Joby to compose a new score for Hitchcock's silent classic **The Lodger.** He has now completed a second film score for the BFI to accompany their release of the silent **The Dying Swan.**

Joby's classical commission for the BBC Philharmonic Orchestra, **Luminescence** was premiered in 1997 under Sir Peter Maxwell Davies. The following year, Evelyn Glennie toured his percussion concerto **Incandescence** with the London Sinfonietta.

More recently, Joby has written the music to the Comic Relief animated film, **Robbie the Reindeer in Legends of the Lost Tribe** (CBS and BBC). In 2002 he formed his own band **Billiardman** a performing ensemble who showcased work from his new album **The Dying Swan: Music for 1-7 Players** (Black Box) at the London Jazz Festival and is currently touring the UK.

Hampstead Theatre opened in 1959 in the upstairs room of The Three Horseshoes pub on Heath Street in Hampstead village. James Roose-Evans, the founding Artistic Director, quickly established an eclectic and adventurous artistic policy which holds good to this day.

In 1962 the audience had grown too large for the Three Horseshoes and a 174 seater portacabin in Swiss Cottage, expected to last 10 years, became Hampstead Theatre's new home. This temporary building lasted 40 years until the new theatre, designed by Bennetts Associates, was opened in February 2003 on Eton Avenue.

"Hampstead Theatre pitches itself just right. It knows what it is about, it strikes the right balance between production and performance with clarity and elegance, and it is clever enough not to steal the show"
HUGH PEARMAN, SUNDAY TIMES

Commissioning Policy

Jenny Topper, the current Artistic Director's commissioning policy is built on three central principles: to encourage commissioned writers to identify lucidly and frankly their particular passions; to be courageous and original in their ideas; and to respond with ambition to the formal challenges of playwriting.

Each year we invite the most exciting writers around to write for us. At least half of these playwrights will be emerging writers who are just hitting their stride; writers who we believe are on the brink of establishing themselves as important new voices. We also ask mid-career and mature playwrights to write for us on topics which have become crucially important to them.

Supporting Hampstead Theatre

Luminaries

By becoming one of Hampstead Theatre's **Luminaries**, you will be giving vital support to all aspects of our work, not just the plays on stage but our education work and audience development initiatives.

There are three levels of support and benefits, starting at £250 a year.

Our current **Luminaries** are:

Level 1
Anonymous
Regina Aukin
Deborah Buzan
Richard Curtis
Robyn Durie
Mr & Mrs Robert Freeman
Linda Goldman
Elaine & Peter Hallgarten
Lew Hodges
Dr A Horwell
Patricia & Jerome Karet
Marmont Management Ltd.
Trevor Phillips
Tamara & Michael Rabin
Barry Serjent
Louisa A Service
Lady Solti
Simon Stapely
Hugh Whitemore & Rohan McCulloch
Dr Adrian Whiteson
& Mrs Myrna Whiteson
Peter Williams
Debbie & Derek Zissman

Level 2
Dorothy & John Brook
Charles Caplin
Professor & Mrs C J Dickinson
The Mackintosh Foundation
Michael & Olivia Prior
Anthony Rosner
Judy Williams

Level 3
Richard & Penny Peskin

Corporate Partners

Hampstead Theatre is proud to launch its brand new **Corporate Partners** scheme. This gives a flexible package of benefits to entertain your clients, help promote your business objectives and take advantage of everything the new theatre has to offer. A Corporate Partnership is available from £5,000 + VAT.

We also offer a range of sponsorship opportunities, including performance and production sponsorships, support for education projects or other initiatives at the theatre.

Our **Corporate Partners** 2003 / 2004

Bennetts Associates Architects

To find our more, contact our Development Department on 020 7449 4160 or email development@hampsteadtheatre.com

Capital Campaign Supporters

Thank you to all of those who helped us build the new theatre.

Archangels

The Dorset Foundation
Michael Frayn
John McFadden
The Weston Family
The Rose Foundation

Seraphim

The Andor Charitable Trust
William & Midori Atkins
Sir Trevor & Lady Chinn
David Dutton
Harbottle & Lewis
Jacqueline & Jonathan Gestetner
Sir Eddie Kulukundis OBE
John Lyon's Charity
The Monument Trust
Daniel & Elizabeth Peltz
Peter & Wendy Phillips
RAC plc
Paul & Claire Rayden
The Rayne Foundation
The Archie Sherman Charitable Trust
Barry & Laura Townsley

Angels

Michael Codron
Morven & Michael Heller
Mr & Mrs David Mirvish
The James M Nederlander Foundation Inc
Hilary & Brian Pomeroy
The Family of Alexander Sarner
White Light
The Harold Hyam Wingate Foundation

Cherubim

The Acacia Trust
Anonymous
The British Land Company PLC
The John S Cohen Foundation
The Noel Coward Foundation
David Day
David & José Dent
The Equity Trust Fund
Joyce & Norman Freed
Hampstead & Highgate Express
G Laurence Harbottle
Sir Maurice & Lady Hatter
Debra Hauer & Jeremy King
Mr & Mrs Marc Hauer
Homevale
Max & Janet Jacobs
Peter & Colette Levy
The Mackintosh Foundation
Nyman Libson Paul
Midge & Simon Palley
Barrie & Catherine Pearson
Peters Fraser & Dunlop
Fiona & Gary Phillips
The Presidents Club
Patricia & James Rothman
The Rubin Foundation
Anthony & Beverley Silverstone
The Steel Charitable Trust
The Stone-Mallabar Foundation
Tom Stoppard
Caroline & Simon Tindall
The Trusthouse Charitable Trust
Della Worms & Fred S Worms OBE

We would also like to thank all of those who have named seats in the auditorium, and contributed via telephone and local appeals.

Education & Participation Programme

Since its inception in 1998, we have had over 58,000 attendances from writers and actors aged 5 to 85. Now based in **The Space**, a flexible performance area in the new theatre, local residents and schools are encouraged to make use of the Theatre's expertise and facilities through a number of different projects: **Ignite**, an extensive programme of education and community outreach projects; **The Heat and Light Company** – open to ages 13 – 18 and a thorough introduction to all the essential skills that make theatre; an adult writing and drama course, **Generator** – available to everyone over 18, whatever their experience or ability; and **Nova** – for first time writers aged 55+.

To find out more visit our website, talk to us on 020 7449 4165 or email education@hampsteadtheatre.com

Priority Supporters

With advance information and priority booking you can be the first to discover fresh and dynamic playwrights, and make the most of a whole range of discounts for just £12 a year. For more details call us on 020 7722 9301 or email info@hampsteadtheatre.com

Cafébar

Open 9.00am to 11.00pm Monday to Saturday, the cafébar offers a generous selection of sandwiches, baguettes, warm paninis and salads.

Our new building is also an ideal venue for celebrations or conferences. For further details email conferencing@hampsteadtheatre.com or talk to us on 020 7449 4205.

Hampstead Theatre
Eton Avenue
Swiss Cottage
London
NW3 3EU

T 020 7449 4200
F 020 7449 4201
info@hampsteadtheatre.com

www.hampsteadtheatre.com
Box office 020 7722 9301

Charity Registration No 218506
Company Registration No 707180
VAT No 230 3818 91

Peter Wolff
THEATRE TRUST

The Peter Wolff Theatre Trust is delighted to be supporting this presentation.

The Trust was founded by Peter Wolff, a textile entrepreneur, who has had a great love of the British theatre all his life. In January 1998 he created the non-profit-making Trust to encourage the work of emerging British playwrights and to bring these plays to a wider audience.

Among the plays supported by the Trust have been:

John Haynes

AN EXPERIMENT WITH AN AIR-PUMP
by Shelagh Stephenson at Hampstead Theatre

"Bursting with anxieties and bristling with ideas, this is the most infectious dose of millennium fever you're likely to catch this side of 2000" *The Times*

Kevin Low

PERFECT DAYS
by Liz Lochhead at the Vaudeville Theatre

"To see Liz Lochhead's utterly Scottish *Perfect Days* now that it has transferred to London is to see how perfectly made, how broad and how deep, this play is" *The Financial Times*

Marilyn Kingwill

BE MY BABY
by Amanda Whittington at the Soho Theatre

"*Be My Baby* marks the birth of a strong, healthy new dramatic talent" *The Independent*

Henrietta Butler

TO THE GREEN FIELDS BEYOND
by Nick Whitby at The Donmar Warehouse

"Nick Whitby's play is saltily written and emotionally affecting" *The Guardian*

Manuel Harlan

SPLENDOUR
by Abi Morgan with Paines Plough

"It is Abi Morgan's *Splendour* that seems to do more to push new writing by women, about women, into a new century" *The Scotsman*

HUMBLE BOY
by Charlotte Jones

Originally presented at the National Theatre. Transferred to the West End in 2002 and to New York in 2003.

Catherine Ashmore

TAMSIN OGLESBY

US and Them

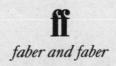

faber and faber

9.99

First published in 2003
by Faber and Faber Limited
3 Queen Square London WC1N 3AU

Typeset by Country Setting, Kingsdown, Kent CT14 8ES
Printed in England by Mackays of Chatham plc, Chatham, Kent

A CIP record for this book
is available from the British Library

ISBN 0–571–22129–7

2 4 6 8 10 9 7 5 3 1

Characters

Ed Marshall
American (New York) businessman.
Late forties. Lori's husband

Lori Marshall
American. Late forties. Ed's wife

Jay
Their son, twenty-one. Musician

Charlotte Gardner
English. Mid-forties. Linguist. Martin's wife

Martin Phillips
English. Forty. Inventor. Charlotte's husband

Izzie
Their daughter, nineteen. Economics student

*The following characters are all played
by the same actor*

Waiter
Japanese. First-generation immigrant to the US

Maynard
Musician

Timothy
Oriental-American architect

*The action takes place between New York
and various locations in England*

Act One

A plush New York apartment, Upper East Side.
Charlotte and Martin are ushered in by Ed and Lori.

Charlotte I'm fine, no, I'm absolutely fine now, just
watch my face and tell me if I go green because I usually
go completely green just before I throw up. But to be
honest I don't think there's anything left. I was sick at
the Met this morning, thought, oh I feel better now, so
off we went downtown to Lucca's, I mean all I had was
soup, and I was perfectly all right until I got outside and
vomited all over the menu board.

Ed You're not pregnant?

Charlotte Are you joking?

Ed Yes.

Lori Are you sure you're all right?

Martin She's fine.

Charlotte Apparently I'm fine.

Lori What do you think it was?

Martin / Alcohol.

Charlotte Food poisoning. Well, I am slightly allergic to
alcohol. As you know.

Lori But what did you eat?

Charlotte Prawns.

Lori Ah.

5

Charlotte Exactly, but the thing is, every time I have them I also seem to drink too much, so –

Ed Well, we're glad you could make it. But if we'd known, we could have re-scheduled.

Charlotte No, we got your message and thought, you know, haven't seen you for days, you're busy, I mean we're all so busy, isn't it ridiculous? But we're not over for much longer, so, you know –

Martin So what's it all about?

Ed Excuse me?

Martin You said, in your message, you implied, you had some kind of announcement to make.

   Ed starts to open a bottle of champagne.

Ed Let's just settle down and relax a minute. There's no hurry.

Martin Oh, not champagne again.

Ed I'm sorry. Would you / like something else?

Martin Of course not, I'm just kidding. I love champagne.

Charlotte Kidding.

Martin What?

Charlotte Giving birth to a goat. Taking a goat for a walk?

Martin She's off.

Charlotte I'm not aware of you ever having used that phrase before.

Martin I've used it all my life.

Charlotte You've done it all your life. But the phrase is American.

Martin We're in America.

Charlotte It's not a criticism.

Lori offers them pistachios.

Lori Pistachios?

Martin So, where are we eating?

Pause.

Charlotte Are we eating? Maybe we're not eating.

Martin Go on. Tell us what it is.

Pause.

Charlotte *You're* not pregnant, are you?

Lori No.

Charlotte Now that would be something.

Lori Not something to celebrate, though. Except maybe on behalf of science.

Martin It's a celebration, then?

Lori No.

Ed No. Not a celebration, no.

Martin Oh.

Charlotte Something about Jay?

Lori No, but apparently he has a girlfriend.

Charlotte Fantastic. So has Izzie. A boyfriend, I mean. Haven't met him yet, though.

Lori Needless to say, neither have we. But I'm told it's serious.

Charlotte So, it's not a celebration. (*Pause.*) A funeral? Has somebody died? Please don't tell me somebody's died.

7

Ed Nobody's died.

Charlotte Animal, vegetable or mineral? Oh God, this is making me feel slightly hysterical. You look so serious, the pair of you. (*Pause.*) You're not getting divorced, are you?

Ed No, we're not getting divorced.

Charlotte I'm sorry, I didn't for a minute think you were, really. No, that would be awful, it would be like Tony and Cherie splitting up. The moral fabric of society, torn in half. (*Pause.*) Do I smell of sick?

Ed Listen, first of all, I have to say you're great guys.

Martin Is this it?

Ed You're great guys and we've gotten to know each other pretty well over the last couple of years. And we're still of the opinion that we had when we first met, which is that you are both very interesting and entertaining people. We have a large and, I like to think, broad circle of friends, and all these people are interesting people on their own terms, regardless of their particular social or professional status. We have friends who work in the Post Office, we have friends who own the Post Office, we have friends who work behind bars –

Lori We have friends who should be behind bars.

Ed Exactly, we have friends who work in government, we have friends who don't work at all –

Lori Marsha's never done a day's work in her life.

Ed What I'm saying here is that, usually, and fundamentally, I don't give a damn where you come from, what you do or how much you're worth. And on that basis, we have always believed we had a special relationship with you guys. That we had a connection, despite our apparent differences. However, since your circumstances have changed (and I regret that they have) it appears to have altered the significance of some of those fundamentals. Now, nobody's making any judgements here, but it's a fact that, as human beings, we are all partly defined by our association with one another. And the truth is, when that association starts to impact badly on one side or the other, it's time to question that association, and I'm afraid we have come to the conclusion, albeit with regret, that we don't want to be your friends any more.

Silence. Then Martin begins to laugh.

Martin I've always said, when people say, 'Oh, Americans have no sense of humour,' I always say, 'No, you should meet our friends Ed and Lori.'

Charlotte Martin.

Ed I'm not saying you can't give us a call now and again. We'd be happy to talk to you on the phone. But we just don't think it's appropriate to continue the relationship. As it stands.

Silence.

Lori I'm so sorry.

Ed No, there's no doubt about it. We are sorry.

Charlotte But. What – I don't –

Martin You're green.

Charlotte What?

Martin You've gone green.

Charlotte rushes out of the room into the bathroom. Silence.

Ed Would you like another glass?

Martin Let me get this right. Are you saying you don't want to associate with us any more because – what are you saying?

Ed I want you to understand that I am not throwing down a gauntlet here. I'm not asking you to defend yourselves. And I don't wish to get involved in itemising our disappointments or grievances. I figure there are two value systems going on between us which are not compatible and we should just leave it at that.

Lori offers Martin some pistachios. He ignores her.

Martin Jesusbloodyfuckinghell.

Charlotte returns.

Charlotte I can't. The water in the loo is blue.

Martin stands up suddenly and rushes Charlotte out of the room. Silence.

Ed That didn't go too badly.

Lori Oh, I feel terrible.

Ed I thought, there are two ways this could go. One is with dignity. The other is not.

Lori They haven't gone yet

Ed They've gone. Don't worry. They've gone.

Lori You think they'll call?

Ed Why would they do that?

Pause.

Lori No, right, I guess not.

SCENE TWO

A Japanese restaurant. Charlotte and Martin at one table; Ed and Lori at the other.

Martin I would like you to put yourself in my shoes for a minute.

Charlotte Okay.

Martin She was hysterical.

Charlotte I'm listening.

Martin She was Japanese and she was completely beyond anything you would call rational. What?

Charlotte It's a Japanese restaurant.

Martin I'm just stating a fact. That's what she was, Japanese.

Charlotte Okay, okay. So how old was she? Roughly?

Martin I have no idea. She was Japanese, you know.

Charlotte Will you stop saying that word. I mean, was she a girl or a woman, would you say?

Martin I would say she was about thirty-one.

Charlotte Attractive?

Martin What's that got to do with it?

Charlotte Was she?

Martin I have no idea. She was crying.

Charlotte Okay. So.

Martin So she was shaking and sobbing her eyes out and, look, I was only fifteen minutes late! I couldn't just walk away.

Charlotte I'm not angry with you, Martin. I've just had a whole thing of *sake* on my own, that's all.

Martin She was distressed. But you know, and this is what's so awful about it, I didn't want to be the one, because the first questions you ask yourself are, 'Is she mad?' or, 'Is this a trick?'

Charlotte And was she?

Martin Well, this is it, you see. What she was is claustrophobic. That's all. I mean it was a big deal obviously, for her, she was shaking and crying and all she could say when I asked her what was wrong was, 'Panic attack, panic attack.'

Charlotte Martin.

Martin Will you stop –

Charlotte If I'd known, we'd have gone French.

Martin We didn't want French. And if I'd known I would not have taken the subway and we would not be having this discussion.

Charlotte Anyway anyway anyway. What happened?

Martin What happened was I went to comfort her and this *girl*, she can't have been more than twenty, this girl came up and had a go at me for upsetting the woman.

Charlotte No.

Martin As though I'd started it.

Charlotte Oh, that's not fair.

Martin It's bloody unfair. So we're having this argument, me and the girl, the Japanese woman's screaming, 'Panic attack, panic attack,' and then these people appear out of nowhere wearing air-force-blue uniforms with yellow stripes, and whisk her away.

Charlotte Well, who were they?

Martin I have no idea. Could have been the CIA. She could have been a fugitive for all I know. They could have been minders or ticket collectors or people on their break from the local supermarket, but we just let them take her away, not a word, because they had uniforms.

Charlotte Air-force blue and yellow?

Martin Weird uniforms.

Charlotte They were probably security guards.

Martin Well yes, probably, but, you know.

Charlotte Or Thunderbirds.

Martin I don't know, you try to help someone and what happens?

Charlotte You can't win. Anyway. Hurry up and finish that and we can go to one of those bars I was telling you about where they give you coffee and pudding. You want to see what I bought?

Martin As long as it's not expensive.

Charlotte Don't start.

Charlotte gets out her shopping to show him.

On the other table:

Lori There's a kid in there called Joey and this kid, / I've seen him –

Ed I know, the Mackenzie boy.

Lori – right – he *knows* me, so many times I've seen him, but today he looks at me like I stepped in something bad and then starts, you have no idea why they do these things, but he picked up a toy mallet and started trying to concuss himself with it, I mean really injuring himself.

13

Ed You know I have to say something, honey, and I think you know what I'm going to say, but you're getting *involved*.

Lori You're right, I am. No, you're right.

Ed No, it's entirely to your credit. But if you're going to be an ambassador for these guys you have to stand back a little.

Lori I know, I know, I just feel so useless.

Ed Honey. You're smart. You have beautiful brown eyes. You have the most adorable chin and I love you.

Lori Well, thank you, honey, but –

Ed Don't thank me. Kiss me.

She does.

Lori But other times it's fantastic, other times when they respond to you, it's like, oh God, it's like the sun just came out.

Ed That's good. Because they're talking about a cure, right? They claim they have a cure for this thing, is that right?

Lori It's more like, okay, there was this kid, and what you do, you keep saying, 'How are you? I'm fine. How are you?' You get them to repeat it until the theory is one day they stop being parrots and they become people, and he did it, this kid, he asked me how I was without being asked to ask me.

Ed No, that's more than a certain person in this family will do, so, no, that is not insignificant.

Lori It's significant.

Ed It is. But, another thing. The Mackenzie boy. We have to remember, that is what he is.

Lori What?

Ed The son of a Mackenzie.

Lori Oh, that's not fair.

Ed No, correct me if I'm wrong, but they have not ruled out the hereditary factor in this disease.

Lori Sure, but you know, where does that leave us?

Ed My son is not autistic.

Lori Of course he's not, he's just troubled. Oh, shoot. I didn't mean to bring him into this.

Ed He's not. He is not in this. He is entirely lacking in social grace and communication skills, but he is not in this.

Lori Absolutely.

Ed Absolutely not.

Lori No, absolutely.

Ed Not. The guy is not autistic. He just needs a girlfriend.

An alarm bell goes off.

What the –

Everyone looks about. A Waiter rushes over to Charlotte and points to her coat.

Waiter Is your coat?

Charlotte Oh my God, it's me.

Waiter Is on heater.

Charlotte Of course. Sorry. It must have just fallen –

Waiter It fall on heater.

Charlotte – yes, on the heater, oh my God. Sorry. I'm so sorry.

Waiter Okay. (*He goes.*)

Charlotte How embarrassing.

Martin Is it okay?

Charlotte It's fine. Oh no.

Martin What?

Charlotte There's a burn. It's burnt my sleeve. Look.

Ed Excuse me? Pardon me, but I have to tell you those things are totally illegal in a public establishment. You should ask for the manager.

Charlotte Right. Illegal?

Ed Right.

Charlotte Because . . .

Ed Because of what you saw right there. They're a hazard.

Charlotte Hazard. Of course. A hazard.

Ed Notice he didn't hang around. He's well aware they're in breach.

Martin No, he didn't actually apologise, did he?

Charlotte I just felt stupid because, you know, it did fall off, but then where else was I meant to put it?

Ed You should definitely talk to the manager and show him your coat. You want me to call him? I'd be happy to talk to them. I've seen this kind of thing many times. It's a regulation.

Charlotte Really?

Ed No question.

Charlotte You think I should?

Martin Why not?

Charlotte It's not that bad.

Ed Definitely.

Lori A burn is a burn.

Pause.

Charlotte Okay. I'm not very good at this. (*She puts up her hand.*) Hello? Hello? Excuse me. I'm not very happy about my coat. It's burnt. Could I talk to the manager please?

Waiter Manager not here.

Ed Oh, come on.

Charlotte Someone in charge then.

Waiter Talk to me.

Charlotte Are you in charge?

He nods.

Well, the thing is, I didn't realise before, and I'm sorry I set the alarm off, but when my coat landed on the heater it got burnt.

Waiter Okay.

Charlotte Well, it's not okay, is it, because it's my favourite coat actually.

Waiter What you want me to do?

Charlotte Well, I don't know, I mean, you know –

Waiter You bring receipt.

Charlotte For the coat?

Waiter You get coat cleaned. You bring receipt.

Charlotte It's a burn. It won't wash off.

Martin You cannot clean a burn.

Waiter You bring receipt. We pay receipt.

Charlotte Oh, this is ridiculous.

Ed Look, these portable heaters are illegal. Do you understand?

Waiter But is not – is not – you please – I talk to the lady.

Ed You know as well as I do it is against the law to have these things in a public establishment. Now either you pay the lady's cheque or you buy her a new coat.

Waiter Uh . . .

Ed Listen. (*He shows the waiter his card.*) I could have this place closed down tomorrow. Now either you pay the lady compensation or I call the head of the Building Department Monday morning.

Silence.

Waiter Okay.

Ed Thank you.

Waiter (*to Charlotte*) What you want me to do?

Charlotte Um. Well. If you paid for the meal that would be nice, thank you.

He goes.

Oh, I feel bad now.

Ed No, he's lucky to get away with it.

18

Charlotte I mean, thank you. That was very kind of you.

Ed No problem. (*He holds out his hand to Charlotte.*) Ed Marshall. And this is my wife, Lori.

Charlotte Sorry, Charlotte. Martin.

Lori How long have you been in New York?

Charlotte Oh about five hours.

Lori Oh my God, they've just arrived! Welcome to New York!

Ed You guys on vacation?

Charlotte Yes.

Martin No.

The Waiter arrives at their table.

Ed Hi.

Waiter Please, excuse me, you sign this, please.

Charlotte What am I signing?

Waiter No complaint. You sign here and you will be happy.

Martin Can I sign too?

Ed Sure. It's in the Constitution.

Lori Pardon me, does that say Gardner?

Charlotte Yes, that's my maiden name.

Lori Oh my God.

Charlotte I know, I still use it for some things. I don't know why really –

Lori Nononono, it's *my* maiden name.

Charlotte Really?

Lori Gardner, without the 'e'. It's even spelt the same.

Ed Well, isn't that extraordinary? Have you ever met an *English* Gardner?

Lori No, I never have. Which part of England are you from?

Charlotte Um.

The Waiter is hovering.

Ed Can we help you?

Waiter (*to Charlotte*) Please, you still give tip to waitress, is not her fault.

Charlotte Of course, yes, I wouldn't dream, of course.

Waiter Thank you.

Ed Listen. I'm sorry if I was a little heavy earlier. But you know the food here is excellent. (*Ed shakes the Waiter's hand and puts the tip into it. He whispers in the Waiter's ear and indicates their coats on the other side of the room.*)

Lori It is outstanding.

Charlotte Yes, my meal was delicious, sorry, thank you.

The Waiter goes to fetch their coats.

Martin He probably took it out of his own wages. You're a hard woman.

Charlotte Oh, stop it.

Martin No, I like it. Do you know anywhere else like this? Maybe a nice quiet bar with big inflammable sofas.

Ed Well, as a matter of fact our apartment is just a couple of blocks away.

Lori And we do have a big sofa.

Ed But not a lot in the way of fire hazards.

Lori You're more than welcome to join us for a nightcap.

Martin That's very kind of you. I didn't mean –

Ed No, I insist.

Martin Well –

Charlotte Thank you. We'd love to.

Ed It would be our pleasure.

Martin Thanks.

Charlotte Lucky die.

Lori Excuse me?

Charlotte Die. Means hazard.

Lori Oh.

Charlotte As in dice. It's from the Arabic.

Lori Right.

Martin She's teaches linguistics.

Lori Oh. No, it doesn't sound English at all.

Charlotte Hazzaard.

Ed Would you excuse us a moment?

Lori It sounds ridiculous.

Ed Lori?

Charlotte / Hazaaaard.

Lori Hazaaaaaaard.

The Waiter stands to one side with the Marshalls' coats; Ed leads Lori away to put them on.

Charlotte They're so friendly. It's what I love about them, so open. Can you imagine, in England?

Martin No, everyone would disappear behind their menus.

Charlotte They didn't have to say anything.

Martin And the waiter would have said, 'If you don't like it, piss off.'

Charlotte They're so straight. So straightforward.

Martin Direct.

Charlotte And forceful. Did you notice how forceful he was?

Martin Now now.

Charlotte What?

Martin Well, he was getting his dick out, wasn't he?

Charlotte He was not! How can you say that? He was being nice.

Martin And slapping it on the table.

Charlotte He was standing up for me.

Martin Exactly.

Charlotte Oh shut up stop it that's enough. I like them.

Martin I'm not saying I don't.

Charlotte A free meal, can you believe it! I will always think well of this coat. Oh my God, look. Oh that's awful.

Martin What?

Charlotte It's not burnt. It's just dirty.

Martin You lied. You humiliated that poor man and took his evening's wages all for nothing. Call him back.

Charlotte I can't call him back. It's too embarrassing. I can't.

Martin He's going to go home and commit hara-kiri.

Charlotte I can't go back after all that.

Martin Well, come on then. Let's get out of here. Quick. Before he realises.

Charlotte What are you talking about?

Martin The Japanese can read newsprint from a distance of up to three miles. Like owls.

Charlotte Oh, fuck off. He's not even looking.

Martin And they can turn their heads two hundred and seventy-five degrees in both directions.

Charlotte Maybe I'll come back tomorrow.

Martin Forget it. Come on.

They start putting on their coats. Ed and Lori wait to one side.

Lori Why, what a delightful couple.

Ed Charming.

Lori No, they're really charming.

Ed The thing about the British, once you prise them out of their shells it's always a pleasant surprise to discover that they are in fact warm-blooded mammals.

Lori We should introduce them to Clare and Robert.

Ed yawns.

Ed I would imagine Martine's. There's nowhere else round here.

Lori Oh, honey, you're tired. Was I wrong to ask them back?

Ed It's not an issue. Anyhow, I asked them back. Do we have tea in the apartment?

Lori Of course we have tea. Why wouldn't we have tea?

Ed That's good.

Lori We have English Breakfast and we have afternoon tea.

Ed No, that's fine.

Lori But we do not have evening tea and I have no tisanes. Is Breakfast tea too strong?

Ed The strength is immaterial. But an absence of tea would upset them. The important thing is, they have the choice.

SCENE THREE

The Marshalls' apartment. Silence. Martin and Charlotte stare around the room.

Charlotte Fuck.

Martin They're rich.

Charlotte They're fucking loaded.

Martin Don't tell them why I'm in New York.

Charlotte Why not?

Martin Because they'll think we engineered it. Coming here.

Charlotte We didn't.

Martin But they'll *think* we did.

Charlotte Well if we'd known they were loaded we would have done.

Martin Look. Just because they're rich doesn't mean they have money.

Pause.

Charlotte Yes it does.

Martin Charlotte. I am not going to go asking the first person we meet for money. I have meetings with investors already lined up, and we don't know anything about them.

Charlotte Do you think this is genuine?

Martin Course it is.

Charlotte God.

Martin My grandmother had loads of them.

Charlotte (*she examines a painting*) And what's this, who's this by, then?

Martin Don't know, don't like it. It's too dark.

Charlotte You're too dark. I like you.

Martin Don't drink any more, all right? Because you may not feel it, but you are drunk and Americans don't drink, they control themselves.

Charlotte Well I'm not having any more of that tea. It's disgusting.

Martin We've just met them and I don't want them to think – I don't want them to think of us like that.

Charlotte Like what?

Martin Like people who can't stand up after one bottle of *sake*.

Charlotte Oh Martin, I feel a bit sick.

Pause.

Martin Shall we go?

Charlotte What, just leave? We can't.

Martin We can.

Charlotte They're nice people. I like them.

Martin We don't know anything about them. They could have brought us here for sex. Or drugs. Oh God, your eyes are starting to cross. How many noses have I got?

Charlotte Five.

He starts blowing in her face.

Martin Look at me look at me look at me, okay, concentrate on my finger.

Lori enters with a book, followed by Ed with tea and cookies.

Lori I found it, look, my great-grandmother wrote this journal on the passage over and she says here, oh, where is it? Uffingham. No, Offingham. In Gloucestershire. That's where they're from. Do you know it?

Charlotte No.

Lori You must be on a different branch. Herefordshire? Did you say your mother was from Herefordshire?

Ed She's probably on a more refined branch of the tree.

Lori Oh, sure she is. My English ancestors are nothing to boast about. Previous to coming here, the only one we had who made it was a guy called / William Gardner, who was very –

Ed Bill Gardner.

Lori – successful in the military.

Ed Well, he was actually an advisor to King Charles I, although he died in a manner which suggests his advice was not appreciated. I'm sorry, you must be exhausted. But there's no point in going to sleep now. You have to stay up all night. Do you take drugs?

Pause.

Martin Drugs?

Ed I always take Transzone when I fly long-haul. Knocks me out.

Martin I have no trouble falling asleep anywhere, I'm afraid.

Lori I know what you mean, but Ed and I like to take it in turns and watch.

Martin I'm sorry?

Lori One of you sleeps while the other watches over you. In case you dribble.

Martin Of course.

Charlotte Oh, he's hopeless. He was sitting there, on the flight over, one minute he was sitting there with a plate of coronation chicken, the next minute I looked up and he was fast asleep with his head in the lap of a woman who was reading Balzac.

Ed Ah, the civil wilderness of sleep.

Charlotte But you could have fallen on my shoulder, couldn't you? What can I say? He has a natural predilection for strangers.

Ed Well, that's lucky for us. Would you like some more tea, Charlotte?

Charlotte No. Thank you.

Martin I'd love some, thank you.

Lori It's not too strong?

Martin It's perfect.

Ed So how old is your daughter?

Charlotte Nineteen.

Ed Jay's twenty-one.

Charlotte Your son?

Ed That's just great?

Martin Shall we set the wedding date now or do you think we should wait?

Ed No kidding. What's the dowry?

Martin Oh the usual. Couple of goats and some olive oil.

Ed It's a deal. If she's anything like as charming as you guys.

Martin What do you think, Charlotte? Charm is not perhaps the first word that springs to mind.

Ed No, Jay is a great guy. I'm sure he would love to show your daughter round.

Lori Where is she now?

Charlotte Asleep.

Ed Big mistake.

Martin No, really, we should join her. In our own beds, of course.

Lori It would be good for Jay to meet someone new. Wouldn't that be great if they got on?

Ed I'm sure they will, honey, why wouldn't they?

SCENE FOUR

Jay's room: Izzie watches Jay, unobserved, while he sits at his music deck, mixing. He makes various adjustments and suddenly notices Izzie. He turns off the music abruptly and stands, awkwardly.

Izzie S'all right, mate, no, you carry on. I'm cool. I just thought if I tap him on the shoulder he might, you know, pull a gun on me or something, I don't know. But, I'm not being funny, right, but I've got a mate who's a DJ, looks a bit like you. He's got this really big head and muscles like Arnie, but the rest of him is thin as piss, so when he stands up he looks like a fucking lollipop.

Jay I'm not a DJ.

Izzie Yeah, we used to be in this band together. I mean, I wasn't anything. I was one of the floozies up the back going doowop. It was fantastic. But we were crap.

Pause.

Jay I can believe that.

Izzie No we were, we were like so not good. Which was all right, 'cause, you know, it was like, just a laugh really – what did you say?

Jay Who are you?

Izzie You know who I am. I heard your dad telling you who I am.

Jay I haven't listened to anything he's said in years.

Izzie Yeah, right. Izzie. And you're Jay.

Silence. Jay just stares at her, unnervingly.

Are you on something?

Jay No. Are you?

Izzie No. 'Course not. It's what they always say, innit? You're just feeling a bit, you know, hooty, they go, 'Are you on something or what?' It's like my mobile's off for five minutes, they think I'm scoring heroin.

Jay Life is weird enough without drugs.

Izzie notices someone out of a window.

Izzie There's a bloke waving at me.

Jay So wave back.

Izzie I don't know him.

Jay I don't know you.

Izzie Jesus, I'm only being polite. I could be up the Empire State Building.

Jay I'm not stopping you.

Izzie I thought Americans were meant to be friendly.

Jay I thought the English were meant to be reserved.

Izzie Oh, right. Like the Queen. Or Julie Andrews. Or what? Like I suppose like you think we all like lying down and saying please walk over me and sorry for the inconvenience but would you be so kind as to get off my fucking foot? Like we're all frigid but enjoy being spanked? Like we go around drinking tea and eating scones and digging herbaceous borders all day? Like we're all a bunch of losers? Like we all hate Americans? Anyway, I'm not *English* actually. My mum's from Ireland and my real dad's half-Danish.

Jay So how come you sound like you have an alien object stuck up your nose?

Izzie I was just born there, right. And, like, brought up there. (*Pause.*) I'm sorry, but what is your problem?

Split scene.

Ed and Martin in Ed's office.

At the Pedicurist: Lori and Charlotte sit, trousers rolled up, with their legs ankle-deep in basins of water:

Lori We never argue.

Charlotte No, nor do we really.

Lori We disagree, naturally.

Charlotte Oh of course we . . . all the time we do.

Lori But argument wears away the fabric of a relationship.

Charlotte Absolutely. Never let the sun go down.

Lori 'Do not let the sun go down on your anger. And do not give the devil a foothold.' Ephesians 4, verse 26.

Charlotte It's from the Bible? I didn't know it was from the Bible. (*Pause.*) So what do you do? When you disagree.

Lori You listen to their point of view. You try not to interrupt each other. I think that's important. Remember the other person has their story too. 'Describe' is the key word. You can describe how you feel without insulting them. We often do this thing where we make a list of all the issues as they arise. And then we just have . . .

Charlotte Sex.

They laugh.

Lori As a matter of fact Ed has very little interest in sex. Which I personally find a relief after the sixties. Because you know what? You go for a jog round the park, say half an hour – and you release more endorphins than you would do if you had a multiple orgasm.

Charlotte Really?

Lori Absolutely. Or even just a fast walk. How old are you? If you don't mind me asking.

Charlotte Forty-five.

Lori Oh, that's a good age. I've been forty-five a few years now.

Charlotte Well, but you look younger than me.

Lori Are you crazy? You look like you just popped out of an egg.

Charlotte I feel like I just popped out of an egg.

Lori Isn't it great? And Martin? How old is he?

Charlotte Oh, he's younger than me.

Lori Did he have an unhappy childhood?

Charlotte I'm sorry?

Lori Because they say, don't they, that the greatest gift you can give an artist is an unhappy childhood.

Charlotte He's not an artist.

Lori I mean, I know Jay isn't an artist exactly but he is temperamental and he used to be very good at drawing until he got into computers, but he likes to pretend he had a terrible childhood. I once heard him tell the mother of a friend that he was adopted and that his real mother was a Norwegian opera singer. I know it's strange that I'm so dark and he's blond, but he doesn't even like opera. And sometimes I think, well maybe he *is* adopted, you know, giving birth is so traumatic and I had such a cocktail of drugs, I thought, well, maybe somebody switched him while I was writhing on the operating table. I don't mean to criticise him, he's a lovely boy and on many levels we do have a good relationship. He just never talks to us.

Charlotte Oh, we have the opposite problem. Izzie never stops talking.

Lori He is an artist. I thought you said he was an artist.

Charlotte Well, I mean, he's great at drawing. But he's actually an inventor.

Lori Okay. (*Pause.*) So what do you think is the greatest gift you can give an artist?

Pause.

Charlotte Money.

In Ed's office:

Martin You don't even have to go into the garden.

Ed Okay.

Martin It's all done by remote control.

Ed Go on.

Martin You can relax in the comfort of your home, just program the whole thing and sit back with a pint and a packet of crisps.

Ed Okay. So let's play devil's advocate a minute here. Because it has always been my understanding that the smell of freshly cut grass is one of the greatest aphrodisiacs for the soul. The advent of spring and so on.

Martin There's nothing to stop you opening the door. You know what I mean, you don't *have* to stay inside. You can stand in the middle of your lawn and watch it, you can play a round of golf, go to church, you can go and have sex, you can have sex *on the lawn*, you can do what you like, because the point is you're liberated from the physical act of mowing, which, as my research testifies, is what people like least about grass. It's time-consuming and it's cumbersome. And the Sheep is just the size of, well, a small sheep.

Ed Okay, so, and the reason it's a sheep is because / it eats grass.

Martin It eats grass, exactly.

Ed The Sheep.

Martin As in England – pastoral, arable, green and pleasant.

Ed Okay.

Martin But in time, I'm considering developing a number of specialized versions which correspond to the different potential client countries. There are a lot of animals who eat grass.

Ed But England will be the host country?.

Martin Yes.

Pause.

Ed How about hedgehogs? They're English. Or badgers. Everyone loves badgers. They have this quality, this reserved dignity. No, to me they say 'England'.

Martin You see, you're thinking *Wind in the Willows* now.

Ed Right.

Martin Because they're actually amazingly vicious, anti-social and smelly.

Ed Oh.

Pause.

Martin But hey, they have a great sense of humour.

Ed And they don't complain, right?

Martin No, they're not known for complaining.

Ed They're stoic.

Martin When they get squashed, they get squashed. You don't hear much more about it. No badger marches. Nothing.

Ed Not so much as a letter to *The Times*.

Martin But, you know, the real problem with badgers is they don't eat grass.

Ed What do they eat?

Martin Worms, rabbits and wasps' nests.

Pause.

Ed Okay. Let's have a look at the business plan.

Ed puts out his hand; Martin gives him his business plan.

At the Pedicurists':

Lori You know, I can't believe you've never done this before.

Charlotte It's great.

Lori And you haven't even had the foot massage yet. Tell me, what else have you never done before?

Charlotte No, actually, no, I won't have the foot massage.

Lori No, you have to.

Charlotte No, really, I can't.

Lori You don't like having your feet massaged?

Charlotte No, I do, it's just –

Lori I love feet. Much better than sex, don't you think?

Charlotte It's just, I've got something on my foot.

Lori A corn?

Charlotte A verruca.

Lori A what?

Charlotte You know, one of those black spots.

Lori You have a verruca? On your foot?

Charlotte Yes.

Lori But that's terrible.

Charlotte It's all right, / as long as you don't touch it.

Lori They're highly contagious, aren't they? I have no intention of touching it.

Charlotte Only if your foot happened to touch my foot. I think. You can have a look, if you like.

Lori Where did you pick this thing up?

Charlotte Swimming pool.

Lori My God.

Charlotte Don't they have verrucas in America?

Lori Are you sure it's a verruca? I mean, it wouldn't be anything to do with that disease you had? With the sheep?

Charlotte No. It's not foot-and-mouth. It's just a verruca.

Lori I'm sorry, no, but you should really get that seen to. What does your doctor say?

Charlotte She hasn't seen it.

Lori She hasn't seen it?

Charlotte I've only had it a couple of months.

Lori Two months? And she hasn't seen it?

Charlotte If I went to the doctor with a verruca I'd only get put on a waiting list for six years.

Lori This is terrible.

Lori starts rummaging in her bag for her phone.

Charlotte And by the time they got to see me it would probably have dropped off anyway.

Lori We don't even know how it's transmitted.

Charlotte Or I'd have died –

Lori dials a number.

Lori I mean if you can catch it from your foot why can't you catch it from your hand?

Charlotte – not of the verruca, obviously.

Lori Hello? (I mean Friday morning's not the best time, but –) Hello, is that Lianne? Hi, Jennifer, it's Lori Marshall here, I was wondering . . . no, that's quite all right, listen, Jennifer, would it be possible to squeeze a teensie little appointment in with Don some time . . . No, I figure it should only take . . . no, it's a friend of mine, she has some *thing* on her foot, you know one of those . . . absolutely, an emergency, yes . . . yes, well, that's a little . . . tomorrow morning would be fine . . . really? No, that's perfect. Jennifer, you're a marvel. . . . yes . . . I'm extremely grateful . . . no, thank *you*. (*She* *replaces the phone.*) Eleven-fifteen tomorrow morning. Is that okay?

Charlotte That's really kind of you. I mean, thank you. But I haven't got any insurance here and all that.

Lori It's not a problem.

Charlotte I really don't want to be a pain.

Lori And it should only take twenty minutes or so off your schedule.

Charlotte Just like that!

Lori No, we can't have a Gardner hobbling through the city like a cripple.

Charlotte Thank you so much.

Lori You're welcome.

Charlotte Twenty minutes.

Lori Meanwhile, you should just lie back and / relax.

Charlotte Think of England.

Lori England? Why?

Charlotte Why indeed?

Ed's office. Ed is looking through the portfolio.

Ed No, it sounds to me like it has legs.

Martin No, it absolutely doesn't have legs. It's based on a track system. The design's abstract.

Ed I mean the idea.

Martin Of course, sorry. The idea, yes. Good. Great.

Ed Okay, well, I see no reason why we can't take it to Milcam. I have connections with them going way back, and I think this is just the sort of thing might interest them right now.

Martin Milcam?

Ed Yes, they're pretty big around here –

Martin Oh no, I know who they are. It's just I'm sort of committed to the German company already –

Ed But you haven't *signed*, right? You said you guys just had a verbal agreement.

Martin Well, yes.

Ed No problem. Forget Europe. Milcam take this thing up, it'll be out there before those guys get to do the paperwork.

Martin Right.

Ed Good. Okay. So what can you give me in terms of back story, Martin?

Martin Back story?

Ed How it all began. What were the obstacles you overcame to arrive at this point? Et cetera.

Martin Well, I suppose, I think my initial mistake –

Ed Mistakes are always initial.

Martin Right. But my initial mistake was to build from too narrow an investment base. And mostly from the old economy.

Ed You have a garage?

Martin Sorry?

Ed How about we say it all started in your back yard. You gave up a successful career in what – teaching, to start a small garage operation. Something like that.

Martin Right.

Ed We'll work on it. You have any plans this weekend?

Martin Oh, you know, just touristy things.

Ed Sure. We usually relax at the weekend, you know, leisurely breakfast, church, that kind of thing. You're welcome to join us. He's a very amusing guy, the reverend. It's really more like stand-up.

Martin Oh, that's very – thank you, but Charlotte – well, I mean – yes, why not?

Ed What is this, Cyrillic?

Martin Don't worry, that's the foreign section. Here's the English – I mean British – I mean American – you know what I mean.

Ed Leave it with me.

SCENE SIX

The Marshall apartment. Ed, Lori and Jay. Jay takes off his socks and swaps them over during the course of the conversation.

Ed What you have to remember is that Europeans are accustomed to disease.

Lori But the idea of walking around with these black spots all over your feet. It's medieval.

Ed They have a high level of tolerance based on the empirical knowledge that if it doesn't kill you it will eventually disappear. It's called stoicism. / The Greeks, as you know –

Lori I don't care what it's called. It's entirely unnecessary. But you know what? We may actually be related.

Ed You have a verruca?

Lori No, I do not have a verruca. Celia Gardner was born in Herefordshire, but died in my village.

Ed Okay.

Lori So how did she get there? She must have some connection with Charlotte, you see. I found her on the Web.

Ed Does Charlotte know her?

Lori No, she has no idea about her ancestry. And this woman was like a local hero. She took up arms for the poor, apparently.

Ed What does that mean?

Lori Something to do with fighting, I guess. I don't know. No, I'm finding this research extremely stimulating and rewarding. But then you find these whole branches missing and it can get a little frustrating. I'd have to actually go to England to do this thing properly.

Ed No, you should.

Lori You think?

Ed Sure. We could take a vacation.

Lori Oh, I'd love to go again.

Ed No, I have to tell you they are a very interesting couple. And it looks like Martin and I could do business together.

Lori Well, that's great. And I should get her to meet some of my girl friends. Maybe she'd like to be included in my music circle.

Jay Why?

Pause.

Ed 'Why?' What do you mean, 'Why?' What does he mean?

Lori You know, Jay, they're extremely nice people. (*to Ed*) / I don't think he and Izzie got along.

Ed Why would you ask that question? Why would anyone question common courtesy? Would someone explain that to me?

Lori I don't know.

Ed Okay, so, how many out of ten?

Lori Ed.

Ed No, out of ten, come on.

Lori Darling.

Ed He can count.

Silence.

Jay I should go. I have some . . . things . . . to do, right now.

Ed *I* shouldn't be here. I have *work* to do. But right now, I'm talking to you.

Lori She seemed like a sweet girl. Lovely smile. Like a little Buddha.

Ed So maybe you have high standards. That's good, that's okay. Because, and I want you to know this, your mom is a straight ten and always has been. I have no problem with high standards. But before you go making judgements maybe you ought to consider what your rating might be on the charm scale.

Pause.

Jay Buddhas don't smile, Mom.

Ed If you are not able to engage with this subject in a mature fashion, I think you should go.

Jay goes.

And did you see what he was doing with his socks?

Lori He swapped them.

Ed He swapped them over. I mean, is there a difference?

Lori Maybe there's a left and a right. Some socks – I don't know.

Ed There is no difference.

Lori No, you're right.

Ed Socks are socks. He's insane.

Lori He's troubled. (*Pause.*) I have seen Buddhas smile though. I swear I have.

SCENE SEVEN

A sidewalk. Izzie, Martin and Charlotte are about to enter a café.

Martin I just don't want – I did not come to New York to watch you have your verrucas removed.

Charlotte You're not invited to watch. I was just telling you. It'll only take twenty minutes or so out of our shedule.

Martin *Sche*dule.

Charlotte Whatever.

Izzie stops short.

Izzie I'm not going in there.

Martin What? It's just a café.

Izzie It is not just a café. / That's the trouble with you.

Charlotte Oh, Izzie darling.

43

Martin It sells coffee. That's enough for me.

Izzie It's a chain, all right? It's a huge multi-national whose profits exceed those of the combined GDP of Nicaragua, Kenya, Namibia and Chad.

Martin Oh God.

Izzie You buy coffee in there and you're contributing to the economic destruction of entire countries.

Charlotte We can go somewhere else. There, look, we could sit outside over there.

Martin It's Italian. It's probably a front for the Mafia.

Izzie Oh, please.

Martin And the coffee might be shite.

Izzie Don't be stupid, they invented coffee.

Martin Oh right, like they invented sex? They didn't *invent* it, they're just good at it.

Izzie There you are, then.

Martin Okay. All right. So what happens when they start flirting with you? They're Italian, they're not globally neutered eunuchs. If you get lairy I'm walking out.

Izzie Martin. Flirting I can cope with.

Martin Jesus, your principles are arse over tit.

Izzie walks over and sits down at an outside table next door. Martin and Charlotte join her.

I didn't even know you had a verruca. I mean, how much is it going to cost? / Have you any idea –

Charlotte I don't know, I don't know. I couldn't very well say we can't afford it, could I?

Martin Why not?

Charlotte Maybe she'll pay.

Martin Why should she do that? (*She shrugs. Pause.*) Well they can bloody well afford it, can't they?

Charlotte That's what I mean.

Martin That's different, you see. I mean, that's completely different. If they're going to re-organise our entire lives then they should jolly well pay for it, shouldn't they?

   Silence.

Izzie Do I look English?

Martin No.

Izzie What do I look?

Martin Satanic.

Izzie And I thought they were supposed to like our accent, anyway.

Martin Depends on your accent.

Izzie What's wrong with my accent?

Martin Which one?

Charlotte Oh, stop it, you two.

   Pause.

Martin I thought we might go to church on Sunday.

Charlotte What?

Martin They invited us along.

Charlotte You hate church. You never go to church. We have never been to church.

Martin Calm down.

Charlotte I'm not going. Did you say we'd go? I hope you didn't say we'd go because I'm not.

Martin Just calm down, will you.

Charlotte Suddenly you just say, 'Would I like to go to church?' like it's a concert or a play or something.

Martin Apparently the vicar's very entertaining.

Charlotte I mean, what denomination is it? Are they Catholic? They might be Seventh Day Adventists.

Martin No, that's a lower-class thing.

Charlotte They don't have class in America.

Martin Black, then.

Izzie Jesus Christ.

Charlotte Or Christian Scientists. They might be Christian Scientists. No, lots of apparently normal people are. / Tom Cruise –

Martin Look, I'm not asking you to believe in it, I'm just saying he's very interested in the Sheep.

   Pause.

Charlotte Really?

Martin Yes.

Charlotte You're joking?

Martin No, Charlotte, I'm not.

Charlotte You mean someone's going to invest in it?

Martin I mean, *yes*, I mean he's interested. And he has money to write off.

Charlotte My God. But that's fantastic

Martin Yes, actually, it is. It would be. We'll see.

46

Silence.

Charlotte Can't we just say we're atheists?

Martin No.

Charlotte Why not?

Martin That's like admitting you're a communist.

Charlotte But I'm not a communist.

Martin Look, it's no big deal. Everyone goes to church in America. It doesn't mean anything.

Charlotte And what happens if we have to take communion?

Martin No one can *make* you take communion.

Charlotte I might be the only one left sitting in the pew.

Martin Just say you're feeling hung-over. Just say you were off your face last night and if you have one more drop of wine you'll vomit. It doesn't matter. Being there is what matters.

Silence. Izzie stands up.

Izzie What do you want?

Martin A little respect.

Izzie It's self-service.

Charlotte I'll have a cup of tea, thank you, darling. Do you mind?

Izzie What do you want?

Martin Yeah, coffee.

Izzie goes.

What's she like then? Lori?

Charlotte Nice.

Martin Good.

Charlotte But she's obsessed with sex.

Martin Sex?

Charlotte Obsessed with it.

Martin In what way?

Charlotte In every way.

Martin She's obsessed with sex in every way?

Charlotte Mmm.

Martin God. She doesn't look it.

Charlotte I know. What does she look?

Martin Nice.

Charlotte I don't mean in a crotchless panties and leather way.

Martin No, no.

Charlotte She just kept going on about it.

Martin Right. (*Pause.*) Are you winding me up?

Charlotte What?

Martin Because I'm going to be looking at her now, aren't I, and all I'm going to be able to think is crotchless panties.

Charlotte Oh Jesus, I wish I'd never mentioned it now.

Martin So, okay then, right, you go and get your feet done. I take Joan of Arc shopping. Then what?

Charlotte I thought I might go for a jog round Central Park.

Martin You never jog.

48

Charlotte Or maybe just a fast walk. Well, I've never been to New York before.

Martin So, what, you're going to start shopping all night and roller-blading down Madison Avenue?

Charlotte I'm just integrating.

Martin You're not. You're being annoying.

Charlotte Look, if we're going to be over here half the time I don't want to be an outsider, do I? I want to integrate. And integrate comes from the same root as integrity which is something we could all do with a bit more of, you know, candour, principle, coherence, wholeness. I like Americans. They have those things.

Martin You've only been here a week.

Charlotte And please don't talk to me like that.

Martin Like what?

Charlotte Like, 'You're being annoying,' in that snipey way.

Martin You want to integrate, go to church with me.

Charlotte Oh Jesus.

Izzie re-appears. Without any drinks.

Izzie We're going.

Charlotte What happened?

Izzie The cappuccino machine's broken.

Charlotte Oh dear. Can't you just have a milky coffee?

Izzie No.

Martin Why not? You could blow the bubbles yourself, couldn't you? All it is is coffee, milk and hot air.

Izzie goes. They follow.

49

SCENE EIGHT

Martin and Charlotte's apartment: small and basic.
Ed, Lori and Charlotte enter. Lori keeps her coat on.
Ed tries to help Charlotte off with hers, before removing
his own.

Lori No, I'm sorry, I thought the reverend was very good.

Ed No, he wasn't on form today. This is a man who once managed to get Liza Minelli and Vietnam in the same sentence.

Lori I thought his sermon was very informative. I had no idea the Garden of Eden was in Iraq. It was interesting, don't you think?

Charlotte Yes. I thought the music was wonderful. And who was that woman with the dark glasses?

Ed That was Donna Mitchum.

Charlotte Is she famous?

Ed No.

Lori Actually, she is, she has a very reputable boutique in the Village.

Charlotte Ah. That explains the fancy dress.

Lori Oh, she's excellent. I have a suit from her.

Charlotte And the one who read the lesson or whatever you call it. She looked familiar.

Ed That's the woman who presents the late-night horror show. What's her name?

Charlotte No, Ed, / Ed?

Lori How would I know who presents the late-night horror show?

Ed That was her.

Charlotte / That's my cardigan.

Lori How do you know who presents the late-night horror show?

Charlotte Ed.

Ed She's famous.

Lori I don't know her. She can't be famous.

Charlotte Ed. You're taking my clothes off.

In the process of taking off Charlotte's coat, Ed removes more of Charlotte's clothing than intended. Martin appears.

Ed Oh my God, I'm sorry, I didn't realise it was attached. (*He tries to replace the cardigan while taking off the coat.*) This is complicated.

Martin Is there something going on here I should know about?

Ed Yes, your wife and I have been having an affair. She wants us to go off to the Caribbean and start a new life together but I keep telling her that I'm not worth it, am I, honey?

Lori No.

Martin Don't listen to him. He's a better catch than me.

Ed Ah, but your market value's about to quadruple.

Martin Doesn't make any difference. I'm not an alpha male.

Charlotte Don't put up too much of a fight, will you, I might think you care. Won't you miss me?

51

Martin Don't tell me. The face is familiar.

Ed laughs. Martin gestures to Charlotte to follow him out of the room.

Charlotte He loves me really. He's just repressed. What? Oh yes, sorry. Talk among yourselves.

She follows him out. Silence.

Ed You okay?

Lori Sure.

Ed He's a funny guy.

Lori Mmm.

Ed And she's very . . .

Lori What?

Ed Easy.

Pause.

Lori What do you mean?

Ed What do you mean, what do I mean?

Lori Easy.

Ed You know what I mean.

Lori Relaxed?

Ed Relaxed, yes, relaxed.

Lori And I'm not?

Ed I'm not saying you're not relaxed. I'm just saying she *is*.

Lori But you're making a distinction between us.

Ed No, no, I am not making a distinction. I am simply making an observation.

Lori But would you say, okay, would you say I was relaxed?

Ed Not at this moment, no, I would not say that.

Lori Generally speaking, I mean, generally.

Ed Look. I don't want to get into a comparison thing here. You have amazing tenacity and patience and energy. You have incredible energy, I love your energy.

Lori I'm not relaxed.

Ed Are we arguing here? Why are we arguing?

Lori I have no idea.

Martin and Charlotte re-appear carrying a large painting. It is an artistic representation of a herd of 'Sheep' in a beautifully drawn landscape.

Ed What's this?

Martin It's for you.

Lori It's for us?

Martin Just a little, you know . . .

Lori But that's wonderful!

Ed Now that is quite remarkable.

Lori Oh, I love it.

Martin It's just a fantasy landscape really. With the Sheep, you know, in it.

Charlotte So do I.

Ed I told you he's a genius.

Charlotte We just wanted to give you something. As a thank you.

Ed That's a wonderful gift. Thank you.

Martin / Pleasure.

Lori Would you look at that detail.

Martin Was there any response from Milcam?

Ed Oh, they're interested alright. They have to check out the claims, obviously.

Martin Oh, I've done that. I've already done that.

Ed Don't worry, it's just procedure.

Lori You're so clever, Martin. How'd you get to have so much talent?

Charlotte Lori, are you going to take your coat off?

Lori I'm sorry. I wasn't sure if we were staying.

Charlotte Oh no, you must have a drink now you're here.

Lori Actually I think I'll leave it on if you don't mind. My circulation's a little slow.

Charlotte I'll go and see what I can dig out from our little kitchen squat.

Ed Here. Let me give you a hand.

Ed follows Charlotte; Lori stares at the picture.

Lori Jay should see this. He'd love it.

Martin You know there's an animal called a slow lorri?

Lori A slow lorri?

Martin Yeah, it's really sweet. It moves in slow motion. Like this. No, it does.

Lori Why?

Martin No idea. But apparently, at night, it cranks up and goes wild.

Lori Like me, then.

Pause.

Martin Really?

An elevator: Jay and Izzie, going up.

Jay The United States of America is not an island.

Izzie It's a piece of land surrounded by water, innit? What's that, then, if not an island?

Jay A continent.

Izzie Okay. *Big* island. Has it stopped?

Jay Pardon me?

Izzie The lift.

Jay The what?

Izzie The bloody elevator. What's wrong with it?

Jay Nothing's wrong with the bloody elevator. Manhattan is an island.

Izzie There you are, then.

Jay What is your point?

Izzie My point is the only thing we have in common is we both live on an island and we both speak the same language. Apart from that, you might as well be green and scaly.

Jay No, we do not speak the same language. I speak English. You speak a minority dialect.

Izzie Oh shut up. What floor are we on?

Jay Eighty-two, eight-three.

Izzie Keep talking.

Pause.

Jay Do you like Hershey bars?

Izzie No, I do not like Hershey bars.

Jay I thought all English people like Hershey bars.

Izzie Is that the best you can do?

Jay Excuse me?

Izzie Sugar. You think it's the answer to everything, don't you? You stuff it down your fat little children's throats to shut them up in between *The Simpsons* and *The Sopranos* and then go, oh my God, what did we do wrong, when they get hyperactive and gun down their classmates.

Jay Hey hey hey, hold on a minute.

Izzie Oh dear, I forgot to fasten my safety belt.

Jay That's like saying fish and chips are responsible for Northern Ireland.

Izzie Oh, don't talk to me about Northern Ireland.

Jay You said keep talking.

Izzie What would you know about Northern Ireland? You're American. You wouldn't have the patience for Northern Ireland. You'd *invade* it.

Jay Actually a lot of Americans *are* Irish. My father is an eighth Irish. Does that qualify me to have an opinion?

Izzie No. My mother's Irish. Doesn't mean she knows f— all about it.

Jay I thought your mother was a Gardner from Gloucestershire.

Izzie She's adopted, isn't she?

Jay Is she?

Jay steps out of the lift.

Izzie Where are you going?

Jay We've stopped.

Izzie Are we at the top?

Jay We are.

Izzie Don't touch me.

Jay I have no intention of touching you.

Izzie Just hold my hand, will you?

Jay Without touching you?

Jay takes Izzie by the hand and helps her onto the balcony. Izzie can barely look.

Izzie Oh Jesus, no.

Jay You know, you really should have told me you have vertigo before we started up.

Izzie I forgot.

Jay It was you said you wanted to go up the Empire State Building.

Izzie I did not. I said, 'I could be up the Empire State Building if I wasn't talking to you.' It was a figure of speech.

Jay There you are, see, we do not speak the same language.

Izzie Oh my God.

Jay Don't look down.

Izzie Oh my *God*.

Jay Look up.

Izzie I have never in my entire life been so high.

Jay Look over there.

Izzie Where?

Jay The twins.

She looks, and for a moment she forgets her vertigo.

Izzie That's where they were? Wow. It just looks like a big . . . hole.

Jay It feels like a big hole.

Silence. Izzie suddenly reels back.

Izzie Is it moving? It's moving.

Jay The Empire State Building is not moving.

Izzie It is.

Jay You should do therapy.

Izzie No, I just shouldn't go up tall buildings.

Jay Well, what the hell is the point of being in New York?

Izzie You tell me.

Jay You don't like New York?

Izzie No, I do not like New York.

Jay Okay.

Izzie I hate New York.

Jay You can't even *see* New York. You have your eyes shut.

Izzie I can feel it. And it's wobbling.

Jay Open your eyes.

Izzie If I fell off I'd be dead before I got to the bottom.

Jay How can you fall? You cannot fall off the Empire State Building. You can be pushed. But you can't fall.

Izzie Don't talk to me.

Jay 'Talk to me. Don't talk to me. Why don't you talk? Why don't you shut up?' Why don't you close your mouth and open your eyes and just chill out.

Izzie Jesus. You stand there on top of the tallest building in New York with someone who is *wetting* themselves and all you care about is being cool. You think you're so macho, don't you, with your hands down your designer pants, which some poor Taiwanese kid was probably up all night stitching for a handful of stale rice, you just stand there, like a fucking cowboy. You really think the sun shines out of your arse, don't you?

Jay Well, pardon me but it's better than having something stuck up it.

Izzie And anyway John Wayne had a face-lift and was really called Marion.

Jay goes.

No, please don't go. Jay, don't. I can't . . .

Jay You're confusing me with someone who gives a fuck.

Izzie Please no, I love New York. It's just the buildings.

SCENE TEN

Split scene.

Jay's bedroom: Jay working intently on his computer.

*The Marshalls' dining room: the picture of 'The Sheep'
hangs above the dining table. There is no evidence of
food, but several bottles have already been drunk.*

Lori Of course I know *who* the enemy is.

Martin (*drinking*) It's French, right?

Lori I said I don't know *what* an enemy is.

Ed Sancerre. You like it?

Martin It's wonderful.

Lori I mean just because you don't like someone, does
that make them your enemy?

Charlotte An enemy is –

Lori Can't they just ignore their differences?

Ed Honey. We're talking about countries. Not tea
parties.

Lori I know what we're talking about.

Charlotte An enemy is someone who is hostile / to or
who opposes you.

Ed An enemy is someone or something you fear.

Lori No. That can't be right. / I'm afraid of large spaces.

Charlotte The literal definition –

Ed Fear is inimical to friendship.

Charlotte Okay, but –

Ed So the only real enemy is oneself.

Charlotte The adjective –

Ed I beg your pardon. Tell me to shut up.

Charlotte Shut up. The adjective 'inimical' comes from the Latin *inimicus*, meaning hostile, which is an elision of *in* and *amicus*, meaning friend. So, technically speaking, the two words are contingent on one another.

Lori So, what? You have to know someone to hate them?

Charlotte So the concept contains within it its opposite.

Pause.

Martin No, I'm sorry. There's no way they're interested in friendship.

Charlotte Who are we talking about now, Martin?

Martin I don't mean the whole of Islam, obviously.

Charlotte Obviously.

Martin Just the ones with 'cunt' written on their foreheads.

Charlotte Martin!

Martin No, I'm sorry, we all know perfectly well what the enemy is. Whether he's wearing a turban or a suit or a teacloth – no, I'm not being racist, Charlotte – I'm just saying it makes no difference where he's from, the enemy is terror.

Charlotte It's not the sentiment. It's the word. I just don't think it's appropriate.

Martin Well, what word would you use for men who think the more people they kill the more virgins they get to shag in the afterlife?

Lori No, there is no word.

Martin What would you call a dictator who's so obsessed by power that he assassinates anyone who looks at him the wrong way?

Charlotte The President of the United States?

Martin Oh, come on. A murderer is a murderer. An arsehole's an arsehole.

Charlotte Even when he murders people?

Ed Unfortunately we are currently being governed by a man of very little brain in a climate of extreme hubris. But I don't subscribe to the moral relativism which places a low IQ on a par with terrorism or the systematic torture, rape and murder of one's own people.

Charlotte Sure, okay. But I think –

Ed I am, however, uncomfortable with the notion of enforced democracy.

Charlotte Well, the two words / are antonymous for a start.

Martin You can lead a whore to water, but you can't make her think.

Lori No, because if you force people round to your point of view then it's not democracy, is it? Then it's just . . . awful.

Charlotte It's not awful. It's impossible.

Lori Well, no, because people can change, can't they? Oppressed people can become free. Look at Afghanistan. Poor people can become . . . less poor.

Charlotte Yes, but a Kurd can't become a Turk, can they? No, don't look at Afghanistan. A Pashtun can't become a Pakistani.

Lori Well, but anyone can become American.

Charlotte No, Lori, they can't.

Lori No, they can. Democracy means you can choose – you have the freedom to choose who you are.

Ed No. Democracy means you have the freedom to choose who to blame.

Charlotte Okay. But it doesn't give you the right to raise a false alarm, does it? It doesn't give anyone the right to stand up in a crowded theatre and shout, 'Fire!'

Ed Unless there is one.

Charlotte Exactly!

   Pause.

Lori Is there?

Ed What if there's no such thing as an enemy?

Lori Oh, I hate when you do this.

Martin What are you talking about? The whole world hates you. I mean, we don't, obviously, we're English. But everyone else, I mean, you know.

Charlotte (*to Ed*) Go on.

Lori No, I know what you're trying to say, Martin, but . . . and we do realise that some people don't accept what we stand for. We know we're the pariah. It's the price you pay for being a superpower, right? You guys know what that's like because you had an empire once, too. Maybe that's why you're the only ones who really understand.

   Silence.

Ed Let's take what we're doing today. / We're giving thanks.

Lori Arguing.

Martin Yeah, why are we giving thanks?

Ed Yes, why are we giving thanks?

Lori There's a lot to be thankful for, actually.

Ed Okay, well. It started with the Greeks –

Lori Thanksgiving did not start with the Greeks. It started with the Plymouth colony in 1621. Why does it always have to start with the Greeks or the Incas or some other dead people?

Ed I am not apologising for my knowledge of ancient history, Lori. I'm referring to the origin of Thanksgiving. Okay, so once upon a time the Greeks used to offer up their goats to the gods in the hope of a good harvest. So and if the gods liked your goat they would send rain. That was the deal, right. Everyone was happy.

Martin Except for the goat.

Ed But then along comes this guy, Zarathustra, says hey, how about there aren't a whole bunch of gods up there who decide the weather forecast? How about there's only one *real* god, and all the rest are evil bastards intent on killing you and sleeping with your wife while you're out furrowing your fields?

Charlotte Who won't be placated by goats.

Ed Who won't be placated by anything. They're implacable.

Charlotte So the goat's out of a job.

Ed So, yes, the idea of evil has displaced the function of the goat.

Charlotte Okay. So you no longer need to fathom the minds of your enemies because you're convinced they're going to hurt you regardless.

Ed Exactly. And so who should come trip-trapping across the bridge?

Martin The troll?

Ed No, the troll stays under the bridge.

Charlotte You mean evil is the scapegoat?

Ed That's exactly right. The one who hides behind everyone who disagrees with you. And nothing, in the entire history of the world, has succeeded in paralysing intelligence more than the search for scapegoats. The endless, paranoid search for scapegoats.

Pause.

Lori Is that us?

Charlotte No.

Ed At this moment in history, yes.

Charlotte Oh.

Ed We may be flawed. But we are not responsible for the sins of the entire world. And when we make our Thanksgiving, we like to make sure it's a goat lying on that table, and not a scapegoat.

Lori suddenly leaps up.

Lori Turkey!

Martin Now I'm confused.

Lori Oh my God. The turkey!

Lori runs out of the room

Ed She only cooks one meal a year. You know. It'll be fine.

Martin Well, all we have to offer by way of thanks is a sheep, isn't it?

Ed She only cooks one meal a year. You know. It'll be fine. (*He opens another bottle.*)

Martin So, Milcam are definitely not interested, then?

Ed No, but that's not a problem. Anyhow, like I said, it's a good thing to identify the product as strongly as possible with the host nation before going global. England. Sheep. Start small and you've got somewhere to go.

Martin Well, and the Germans are still interested.

Ed Okay, let's sign with them.

Martin You're still on board, then?

Ed Absolutely. Count me in. No, let's go back to your people. We start in Europe, then we expand.

Martin And take over the world.

Ed And take over the world, right. I love this guy, don't you?

Charlotte He's all right.

Jay's room. Jay is startled by Izzie appearing at his side.

Jay Do you want a peanut butter and jelly sandwich?

Izzie Jesus, you are weird. I walk in here and you leap up like one of us is naked and you ask me – like – what kind of a question is that? I just came in to have a bit of a chat, you know, *conversation*, that pathetic substitute for computer interaction that was invented when the first fig leaf fell off. 'Oh my goodness me, what's that, Adam? It's a penis. What a strange shape. What have you got then, Eve? A bush. Oh that's nice. I thought you were the same as me but you're not, are you, you're different. That's interesting.'

66

Jay I only asked if you wanted a peanut butter and jelly sandwich.

Izzie Of course I don't want a peanut butter and jelly sandwich. How old do you think I am? Six?

Jay I'm having one.

Izzie And I only asked what you were doing.

Jay No. You said, 'Masturbating *and* in front of a computer screen will definitely make you go blind.'

Izzie Well. I can't imagine what else you'd be so embarrassed about except pornography.

Jay Then you have no imagination.

Silence. Jay starts making a sandwich.

Izzie So what are you doing then?

Jay Why should I tell you?

Izzie Because if you don't I'll tell your parents you're rubbing yourself up against the furniture.

Jay Bribery is not a good basis for trust.

Izzie All right, okay. Because I asked nicely.

Pause.

Jay Just don't tell them. Okay?

Izzie Why not?

He fixes her with a look.

Okay.

He hands her some headphones.

Jay You have to listen through these.

He sets up a disc on his deck. She listens. Smiles. Nods.
Does a little dance. She removes the headphones.

Izzie It's fantastic. What is it?

Jay It hasn't finished.

Izzie Did you make it?

Jay Did you get to the bit where it goes real quiet?

Izzie How do you do that? Have you got a band? I mean, how / can you have a band?

Jay No. It's just me, right. Just me. I mixed it, I played all the instruments, I made it. But – this is why I don't – this is what annoys me about *people*. You haven't listened to the end.

Izzie Jay. Chill out. I'll listen to the end. I'm just taking a bit of a break, right, to let you know I think you're a fucking genius. I mean, is this what you do in here? Why the big secret? Is it illegal?

Jay No, it is not illegal.

Izzie So why don't you play it? Why don't you send it out, get it aired? I know people in the industry could do something with this.

Jay I'm not interested in that commercial shit.

Izzie Who said anything about commercial? Jesus. Your parents, you know what they think of you? They think you're a total wanker. At least let them hear it.

Jay No way.

Izzie You think they wouldn't like it?

Jay I'm sure they wouldn't like it. And if they did like it, they'd take the credit.

Izzie They'd be proud of you.

Jay I don't need their pride. I don't care what they think.

Izzie No, of course not. Oh, you are such an arsehole.

Jay Or what you think. I don't care what anyone thinks. People always want to be told what to think by people who are older than them or smarter than them or more hip than them. Well, you can stick all that hierarchy shit. I don't need anyone parading me or criticising me or exploiting me; music doesn't exploit anyone; music is an act of friendship.

Silence.

Izzie I know what you are. You're a nerd. You're just a sad one-man band, shut up in your room playing with your imaginary friends so you can totally like avoid reality or the risk that anyone who knows what they're talking about might stand up and say, 'You're crap.'

Silence.

Jay You want to hear the end?

Izzie Bloody give us it here then.

He hands over his headphones.

And if you don't tell your parents, I will.

Jay What?

Izzie Got any Marmite?

Jay Excuse me?

Izzie Never mind.

Lori enters and places a blackened turkey on the table.

Ed It's a little . . . / dry.

Lori Black. It's completely black.

Martin Let's try it. Here. (*Martin tries a piece.*) Gravy's very good at disguising things.

Lori Oh God.

Ed We can dress it up somehow.

Martin Like what? Like this?

> *He tries to make a skirt out of a teatowel for it. Charlotte stops him.*

Lori It's a disaster. The vegetables, everything.

Ed It's okay, honey. Let's not call in the UN just yet.

Lori No, I'm serious, Ed. Where are we going to get another turkey on Thanksgiving?

Ed Next door?

Lori We cannot go next door and ask for a piece of turkey.

Ed Why not?

Charlotte We can just have a sandwich.

Lori I don't believe this.

Charlotte No, really, I'm not that hungry after all those pistachios. Are we?

Martin We could mince the turkey. Add a bit of tomato, mash the potato and you've got a lovely shepherd's pie.

> *Silence.*

Ed We could get a take-out.

Lori Are you crazy? Has everyone gone crazy? This is Thanksgiving. That's like saying I have no family and no friends.

Martin Can we do Thanksgiving without the turkey?

Lori No, you have to have a turkey. You sit down with your family and friends and share the good things in life that have happened to you or that are happening in the world and it's an opportunity to say things you don't ordinarily say.

Martin We don't need a turkey to do that.

Lori We do need a turkey. The turkey is the focus.

Martin I love it when my wife speaks French. She speaks very good French. See. I don't need a turkey.

Lori Goddamn it. This has never happened to me before.

Ed You're getting angry, Lori.

Lori I am not angry. I am upset.

Ed It's okay.

Lori No, it is not okay.

Martin Listen, you know what? Let me tell you something. No, listen. I don't like turkey.

Lori No, you're just saying that.

Martin No, I don't. Do I? I don't even like turkey.

Lori Is that true?

Charlotte Yup.

Lori Oh, that makes me feel worse.

Martin Why?

Lori No, that makes me feel even worse. You were going to sit down in my home and I was going to feed you something you can't even stand.

Martin It's not that I can't stand it. / I just don't particularly like it.

Lori Why didn't you tell me? I could have done something else. What is there?

Martin Goose?

Lori Yes. I could have cooked you a goose.

Martin Cooked your goose.

Charlotte Martin, don't. It's not the time.

Martin What is the time? Mr Wolf?

Ed It's after one.

Martin Dinner time!

Lori Okay, all right. Let's just go. Let's go eat out.

Martin (*to Lori*) Yes, but what about them? (*He gestures to everyone else.*)

    Jay and Izzie enter.

Ed We'd never get anywhere without a reservation. Listen. Let's just have an omelette or something. You've made a fantastic pumpkin pie. We have our good friends here, we have wine, and we're going to have a good time, okay? Okay, honey?

Lori Okay.

Jay Hey, what's going on?

Ed The turkey's burnt.

Jay There's no turkey?

Ed No, there is no turkey.

Jay You're kidding?

Lori THERE IS NO GODDAMN TURKEY.

Jay Are you crazy?

Lori YES.

Ed Okay. Here we have a perfect example of postmodern conservatism. Jay, it is not the end of the world. You're unhappy, go make a burger.

Jay Why didn't you tell me?

Lori I'm telling you.

Ed What would you have done?

Jay Got another one. (*He goes to his room and sits in front of his computer.*)

Ed He has a turkey in his bedroom?

　Silence.

Lori I'm sorry.

Charlotte No, I'm sorry, / I should have –

Lori I'm so sorry.

Ed Hey, it's okay.

Lori No, it is not.

Ed It's okay.

Lori No, it is not okay.

　Silence.

Ed Izzie. You all right?

Izzie I'm a vegetarian.

Charlotte Why don't you go and talk to Jay, darling?

Izzie Because he's an arse.

Ed I like your daughter.

Charlotte I'm sorry. Izzie!

73

Martin She just doesn't care, does she?

Ed No, I think she cares a lot. She wants to change the world, don't you? And she knows it doesn't pay to hang around with a guy who is so entirely devoid of social skills that he can destabilise a perfectly manageable situation on the one day of the year when the only two words required of him are 'thank' and 'you'.

Lori It's my fault.

Ed No, it is categorically not your fault.

Charlotte It's my fault. I said I'd / keep an eye on the bird while you –

Martin No, I was meant to remind you.

Lori No, no, I should have been watching the time.

Ed It's not, no, will you all stop – this is not the Truth and Reconciliation Commission. It's just a burnt turkey.

Izzie What, Mr Marshall, what do you imagine Jay is doing in his room?

Ed Avoiding life.

Izzie Is that what you think?

Ed You tell me. All I know is he's in there, swapping his socks and counting his molars and listening to music.

Izzie You think he's listening to music?

Ed I know he's listening to music.

Izzie What's wrong with music?

Ed Nothing.

Izzie Music can change things. It doesn't exploit anyone. It's an act of friendship.

Ed Look. I love music. I understand what music can do. I invested in an opera house in Chicago when we were recovering from our first miscarriage. If I want to laugh I listen to Boccherini, if I want to cry I listen to Elgar. This is not about music. This is about life and what you make it.

Izzie You think he's a failure?

Charlotte Izzie!

Ed What are you telling me? You are an intelligent young girl and I'm interested in what you have to say.

Izzie You have no idea what he's doing in there because you never go in there and you never go in there because you have no idea what he's doing in there because you're scared it will have nothing to do with you and then you'll have to admit that's what he is, nothing to do with you, and that the only person he's answerable to is himself.

Ed Firstly, I'm honoured that you should take time to notice me at all since one of the worst fears of a man my age is to be ignored by a girl of your age. Secondly, I don't think anybody is only answerable to themselves and I don't think you do either.

Izzie I – well, I –

Ed And thirdly. What the hell is he doing in there?

Pause. Jay re-enters.

Jay Turkey's going to be delivered in five minutes. And the deal is you get everything included. Except the gravy . . .

Lori What are you talking about?

Jay Some place on Lexington delivers turkeys. We just have to make the gravy.

75

Lori You've ordered a turkey?

Jay And trimmings.

Ed Well, I'm . . . What can I say?

Martin Fantastic.

Lori You did that on the computer? Is that what you were doing in there?

Ed That's very enterprising. Well done, Jay.

Jay No problem.

Ed We were beginning to think you were tapping into the White House.

> *Izzie can't control herself. She hits Jay over the head with a place mat.*

Jay Hey!

Charlotte Izzie! God, I'm sorry. She's a vegetarian.

Jay What the hell –?

Izzie Sorry.

Charlotte She gets a bit hypoglycaemic after one o'clock.

Jay Jesus.

Charlotte Izzie?

Izzie I'm sorry, I –

Martin Looks like the wedding's off.

Izzie Oh shut up, Martin.

Martin Okay. It's all right, ladies and gentlemen. Normal transmission is resumed.

Jay What was that for?

Lori So they're delivering a turkey to the front door and I just have to make the gravy. Well, thank the Lord.

Ed No, I'm impressed.

Jay leaves for his room again.

Lori Where are you going now, honey?

Jay To put in for one vegetarian.

Lori Okay. And tell them we have cranberry sauce. And tell them I already made pumpkin pie.

Martin And tell them I love them. Oh God, the thought of roast potatoes and gravy and meat and, oh it's so – ooagh, don't you just love a roast? The potatoes, hard on the outside, soft on the inside, the meat, moist and firm, and the vegetables, little peas which go pop when you prick them, and then the gravy, dipping everything in the gravy, fantastic, like sex in the shower.

Charlotte Martin. You're talking out loud.

Martin I'm starving.

Charlotte Where are you going, darling?

Izzie Toilet. All right?

Charlotte All right.

Izzie exits.

I'm so sorry about Izzie.

Ed Don't be. She's a very bright girl.

Charlotte It's such a shame they're not getting on.

Ed Who?

Charlotte Jay and Izzie.

Ed You think?

Charlotte Such a shame.

Ed You think they're not getting along?

Charlotte I don't know, Ed, is it the acoustics or am I speaking Mandarin?

Ed No. In my experience you don't hit someone over the head unless there's something going on.

Lori Well, sure there's something going on. She can't stand him. Which she is absolutely within her rights to do. He can be a very arrogant young man.

Ed I would not disagree with that statement. He has the capacity, if you let him, to make you feel like you're the last piece of paper on the toilet roll. But it's usually for your qualities people really dislike you, not your faults.

Martin You think she clocked him because she fancies him?

Ed I think she's ambivalent.

Martin With respect, I don't think she knows the meaning of the word. Good is good and bad is bad and anyone sitting on the fence gets electrocuted.

Ed Well, we all start off as Manicheans. She'll grow out of it.

Charlotte She's so prejudiced.

Ed No, she has opinions of her own. That's good.

Martin 'I have opinions of my own. Strong opinions. But I don't –'

Ed Always agree with them.

Martin Thank you, Mr President.

Charlotte She's not always like this. When you come and see us in England you'll see. She's different.

Martin She's worse.

Charlotte It's just, I'm really sorry, because you've been so nice to us, to invite us here today of all days, and well, ever since we met you, really, you've made us feel so welcome.

Ed No, you're very special friends, and it's a great pleasure to have you with us.

Charlotte Thank you.

Doorbell.

Ed That'll be the turkey.

Lori Oh my God, the gravy.

Ed I'll get the door. You get the gravy.

Lori Oh, Ed, I do love you.

She kisses him. They exit their separate ways. Silence.

Martin Fuck.

Charlotte What?

Martin We're going to be rich.

Charlotte If the Sheep takes off.

Martin Sheep don't fly. Turkeys fly.

Charlotte Turkeys do not fly.

Martin They do.

Charlotte No they don't. That's the whole point of turkeys. They don't fly. Hence the phrase, 'It's a turkey.'

Martin Well, let's hope it's not.

Charlotte Let's hope it is. I'm starving. (*Pause.*) I do like them.

Martin Who?

Charlotte Ed and Lori. They're so refreshing.

Martin I love them. I want to marry them.

Charlotte Well, you've already signed a contract with one of them.

Martin And the other one thinks you're her third cousin removed. No, I really think you should tell her.

Charlotte It's too late.

Martin What will she say when she finds out?

Charlotte It's not important. It's irrelevant. Why does everyone think it's so important?

Martin I don't think it's important. I'm just saying it's not true. You're adopted, Charlotte.

Charlotte So?

Silence. Martin starts humming 'If I were a rich man'. Then stops.

Martin Why did he say we all start off as mannequins?

Charlotte He didn't. Manicheans, he said.

Martin What the fuck's a Manichean?

Charlotte Oh, you know.

Martin No, I don't.

Charlotte Someone who believes in good and evil.

Martin Oh, that.

Martin resumes humming the same tune and begins a little dance, as Izzie enters Jay's room, stands directly in front of him and confronts him.

Jay Are you going to hit me again?

Izzie No.

Jay What?

She kisses him.

Oh.

Jay's track plays out.
End of Act One.

Act Two

SCENE ONE

England. Martin and Charlotte's garden in autumn.
A motorised mower, which resembles an abstract sheep,
rolls across the garden, followed by Martin and Ed, who
carries the remote control. It comes to a halt and bleats.
Martin stands, motionless, in despair.

Martin *Milcam!*

Ed Yup. I saw it in the trade magazine.

Martin And it's the same? It's exactly the same?

Ed It's called a Gobot.

Martin A *what?*

Ed Goat-robot, I guess.

Martin Oh fuck.

Ed It's real ugly.

Martin How can they do that?

Ed Unfortunately, since we only had a verbal agreement, they can do what they like.

Martin But they *stole* it.

Ed We don't know that. They may have been developing this thing before they saw the Sheep.

Martin Oh, come on. When did they file? What's their filing date?

Ed No idea. But that's not necessarily the issue here.

Martin Jesus Christ. I thought of it first.

Ed You know, this needn't be a problem, if we can just turn it around –

Martin What are you talking about? It's a fucking disaster. They've stolen my invention. I took it to them, I showed them the pictures, they were interested, then they weren't interested, and now, a year later, here it is! Is that a coincidence? No, it's a criminal fucking offence!

Ed Sure, it sucks. But they're just doing their job. And our job is to work out how to use this thing to our advantage. Because what I'm looking at here looks way inferior to our Sheep.

Martin Five and a half years, wasted. I've just lost five and a half years of my life.

Ed No such thing as losing. Sometimes you win. Sometimes you learn.

Pause.

Martin What?

Ed You're just depressed. You're disappointed. It's understandable.

Martin I'm finished, Ed.

Ed Okay. Listen to me now. You have a couple of options. If your patent issues, you sue them, right? Otherwise you can challenge their patent on the basis that you thought of it first.

Martin Have you any idea – we're talking thousands –

Ed I'm not suggesting it would be easy. Or cheap. But your intellectual-property insurance will cover you if you can prove you invented it before them.

Martin What?

Ed That's what I'm saying. The question of who filed first is not necessarily the issue.

Martin What's intellectual-property insurance?

Pause.

Ed Are you crazy?

Martin No, I'm not crazy I just don't know what intellectual-property insurance is, but I was under the impression there's a morality, no, a *law*, against theft.

Ed Oh. My. God.

Pause.

Martin Look, Ed, I'm sorry about your money –

Ed That has nothing to do with it. I take full responsibility for my investment. (*Pause.*) I just can't believe you don't have insurance.

Martin We had a verbal non-disclosure agreement, the guy said it was confidential.

Ed Martin. There's a bridge in Brooklyn I'd be happy to sell you. 'Said' is not worth the paper it's written on.

Martin Look, it doesn't make any difference anyway. I can't possibly sue them. They're enormous. I'm fucked. End of story.

Silence.

Ed Okay, let's think about this.

Martin *Gobot*, for Christ's sake.

Ed All right. Here's what you should do.

Martin Maybe it was the name.

Ed What?

Martin Maybe I underestimated the negativity associated with sheep.

Ed It has nothing to do with the name, Martin.

Martin Maybe we should have called it 'Rabbit'.

Ed No, we should not have called it 'Rabbit'.

Martin Why not?

Ed Because of the Aztecs.

Martin I don't think many people know about the Aztecs, Ed.

Ed People should know about the Aztecs. They should know that a rabbit was a god of drink and that they had four hundred of them and they drank themselves to death with their rabbits, five million Aztecs, a whole civilisation. Depressed. Disappointed. Dead.

Martin I haven't been invaded. I haven't had another culture take me over. I've just fucked up. Six years! Oh God.

Ed Listen, Martin. Disappointment should be cremated, not embalmed. Now, you're a very talented man. You're still young, fit, healthy. You have a lovely, intelligent wife. And daughter. You have a beautiful house in the country

Martin I hate the country.

Ed I'm sorry?

Martin I hate the country.

Ed How can you hate the country? It's green, it's beautiful, it's quiet –

Martin It's not quiet. It's full of tractors and people dropping in and weather and Tories and shops with stale pastries. I bloody hate the country.

Ed Okay.

Martin I could have carried on teaching. Why did I give up? What the hell was I thinking of?

Ed Look. It's understandable to want to apportion blame, to yourself or others. To construct a narrative. That's good. A narrative is good. But remember, it's you who controls the narrative, right?

Martin I'm broke, Ed.

Ed What are you saying?

Martin Broke. Without money. Finished.

Ed Broke is temporary. 'Poor is eternal. Broke is temporary.' Are you saying you're bankrupt?

Martin I don't know.

Ed Okay, well, let's not get down on our knees and take the vow of poverty just yet. I can give you / the name of a lawyer –

Martin No, no, I don't want any more of your money. Thanks.

Ed I can give you the name of a lawyer who might be interested in your case. If there is a case.

Martin No.

Ed Okay.

Martin No.

Pause.

Ed Well then, it's important you achieve closure. Whether or not that means filing for bankruptcy or just in psychological terms I don't know. Once you've done that you can start over again.

Martin Oh stop it stop it stop it, Ed, it's not fucking Monopoly.

Ed Well, as a matter / of fact –

Martin No, it is not a bloody board game. I have passed Go, I have not collected two hundred, I have nothing on Park Lane, I have nothing nowhere, I have landed on the man with the moustache who says, 'Go to Jail.' GO TO JAIL, ARSEHOLE. THE END. So don't talk to me about 'starting over again', don't try and make me feel better, I don't want to feel better, I want to feel terrible, I should feel terrible, I am terrible. *I'm a failure*. So don't tell me it's okay, because it's bloody not okay.

A long, uncomfortable silence.

She was right.

Ed Who?

Martin I should have stuck to what I know.

Ed Uhuh. If we all did that we'd still be pulling carts.

Martin She's not going to forgive me this time.

Ed Charlotte? Are you crazy? She's a smart woman. She's beautiful, intelligent. Of course she'll forgive you. She loves you.

Pause.

Martin What makes you say that?

Ed She said so.

Martin She said that? To you?

Ed Listen, Martin. We're gonna leave you guys alone a couple of days. Let you take stock. Lori has some lead she wants to chase up in Herefordshire and I have to tell you this research is proving very successful at taking her mind off things right now. But I could take a look at the figures for you when I come back if you want.

Martin presses a button on the remote and recalls the Sheep to him. It bleats and comes to a halt by his feet. He absent-mindedly strokes it.

Ed Martin? (*Pause.*) How does that sound, Martin?

SCENE TWO

A cemetery. Charlotte and Lori. Lori reads from a piece of paper.

Lori William Frederick Gardner. Born 1793. Died 1824. Farrier.

Charlotte Blacksmith.

Lori That means he was poor, right?

Charlotte He wouldn't have been rich, no.

Lori Betsy Edith Gardner. Born 1819. Married Jonathan Hawking in 1842. Now he was just a labourer.

Charlotte What does this mean? Mary Warren (married Thomas Gardner) dsp. What's dsp?

Lori Died childless.

Charlotte What a CV.

Lori Robert Gardner, labourer, Zachary, labourer . . . labourer . . . oh Thomas Gardner, indentured cordwainer . . . pauper. Oh look, here we go. The burial of the said bastard, James Gardner, is, according to the Statute in the Café provided, / liable unto the charity of the Poor House – what?

Charlotte No, no no. You're getting your 'f' and 's' muddled up again. / 'Case' not 'café'.

Lori Okay, but listen. 'Charity of the Poor House. It hath appeared unto us the said justices . . . that she the

88

said Mary Hegley . . . was delivered of a male bastard
child who died on the sixth day of March blah blah blah
burial proceedings of the said bastard child are likely to
be chargeable to the said parish . . . and further, that
Richard Gardner . . . did beget the said bastard child on
the body of her the said Mary Hegley.'

   Pause.

Charlotte Not exactly landed gentry, I'm afraid.

Lori And a bastard child. My God. It sounds so nasty.

Charlotte It's just a definition, Lori, not an adjective.

Lori No, you wait till I tell Ed. He's gonna love this.

Charlotte Oh look. Albert, died the third day of April
aged *seventeen days*. Alice, three years, something, and
then Martha, four, five, the eldest died at twelve years
old. Six of them. All dead. (*Pause.*) Why?

Lori Tuberculosis, scarlet fever, you name it.

Charlotte No, I mean, why is Ed going to love this?

Lori He thinks my family are a bunch of pussycats never
did anything but sit around all day licking themselves.
But these guys were real poor.

   Pause.

Charlotte Hang on.

Lori Which explains why he would have left, of course.
My God, imagine living with all that disease, poverty
and death. What an awful world it must have been.

Charlotte Still is, we still have those things.

Lori No, not like that we don't.

Charlotte Yes we do.

Lori No, we don't have tuberculosis, / the plague, the Black Death.

Charlotte We have AIDS. We have cancer.

Lori But you don't necessarily die of them.

Charlotte Well medicine, obviously, / can cure some –

Lori Cancer, you can go on for years. You get cancer, doesn't mean you have to die of it.

Charlotte No, that's true. My aunt had cancer three times and she died by falling off the pavement.

Lori It's different now. People recover. But if we were born two hundred years ago . . . well if we were born two hundred years ago we'd both be dead by now.

Charlotte Yes.

Lori Our age.

Charlotte Or grandmothers.

Lori I'm not sure which is worse.

Charlotte Lori.

Lori 'It's not how long the journey takes, it's the distance travelled.'

Charlotte What?

Lori It's what my granddaddy used to say. He was the richest, no, he was the third-richest man in Michigan when he died, so every year he'd take us on a pilgrimage to this grubby little shack and he'd go, 'That's where I was born, girls, and don't you forget it,' and then he'd say, 'Remember, it's not how long the journey takes, it's the distance travelled.'

Charlotte Meaning?

Lori We've come a long way.

Pause.

Charlotte We?

Lori We were destitute. We were orphans. We were poor.

Charlotte You are not them, Lori.

Lori Exactly.

Charlotte No. You're rich. And they're dead. They're just dead people with the same name as you.

Lori How can you say that? They're my family.

Charlotte They're not your family, they're your ancestors.

Lori All right, ancestors, they're my ancestors. They might even be yours. We don't know yet – / it might turn out –

Charlotte Don't know what?

Lori If we're related. Celia Gardner came from your village and she was the second cousin of my great-great-great-grandfather. I don't know, I haven't gone back that far yet, / but when I do –

Charlotte You go back far enough, we're all related. We're all related to one of seven earth mothers. What exactly are you looking for, Lori?

Lori I don't know, Charlotte, I'm just looking for connections. I'm just trying to find out more about where I come from, who I am, that's all.

Charlotte Listen. We're all potentially connected. What is significant is how, to whom, and with what you choose to connect yourself, and against what you choose to define yourself. It's the choices you make that determine who you are. Not whether you were born with a silver spoon or a bloody spade in your mouth.

Pause.

Lori Why are you getting angry with me, Charlotte?

Charlotte I'm sorry, I'm not. I just need a cup of tea. I'm sorry. Can we go now?

Lori I'm just trying to understand some things here. Big things.

Charlotte I could do with a bite to eat as well.

Lori I mean – I have never even been hungry.

Charlotte You don't *have* to eat anything, Lori, I'm just saying –

Lori No. No, I have never, in my entire life, been hungry. No one I really care about has died. Or been seriously ill. I've only been to hospital once, to give birth. Both my parents are still alive. 'The said bastard' James Gardner died when he was only six days old. And mine's only twenty-one. (*She lets out a primal howl.*) My baby! I want my baby back!

Charlotte Lori.

Lori (*crying*) Oh God, I'm sorry. It was the word 'bastard' set me off again.

Charlotte He's not dead.

Lori He may as well be.

Charlotte He's in Australia.

Lori Exactly. He's out there, in the world, miles away. Who knows where the next bomb's going to go off? Nowhere's safe any more, Charlotte.

Charlotte He's not dead. He sends you e-mails.

Lori How do I know they're from Jay? It could be someone just killed him and stole his identity and his e-mail address. He could be dead. He just *disappeared*. You have no idea.

Charlotte I'm sorry, I know, / it must be awful.

Lori At least in those days you didn't expect your children to live.

Charlotte He'll be all right, Lori. He'll be fine.

Lori What about me? What the heck am I supposed to do with myself?

Charlotte You have to just concentrate on other things, / like you are.

Lori But everything reminds me of him. You know, I followed a boy once, back home. All the way from Soho to the Meatmarket. He had the same walk as Jay, but his head was shaved. And when he turned round I saw that it wasn't him and I was relieved. I couldn't bear it if he'd shaved his head.

Charlotte Hey, come on.

Lori I just keep asking myself, why us? We're not bad people. Why us?

Charlotte It's not your fault.

Lori Well whose fault is it?

Charlotte Children can be cruel.

Lori Every day I give thanks.

Charlotte Well, that's great.

Lori I pray. I thank God out loud every day when I get up. I just say, I don't know, I just say, thank you for my life, my husband, my country, and my son, wherever he may be. I don't know, I just say that every morning.

Charlotte Good.

Lori It doesn't make any goddamn difference.

Charlotte Lori. He'll turn up soon. Just like he disappeared. He'll just turn up one day and say, 'Hey, Mum, what's for dinner?'

Lori And I'll tell him it's in the garbage and he can stick it up his arse.

SCENE THREE

Izzie's flat. Izzie is working at a computer screen. Jay comes in.

Jay Hi.

Izzie Hi.

Jay Good day?

Izzie Fine.

Jay How were the kids?

Izzie What?

> *She looks at him, smiles. He has her attention now; he kisses her.*

Jay Anyone call?

Izzie Yeah, that big fuck-off record company again.

Jay What'd they want?

Izzie Your soul.

Jay Parasites.

Izzie Yeah, parasites. I said thank you very much for your interest but I see no reason why we should hand over the management and marketing of someone who already has a fanbase of fifteen thousand on the Web alone.

Jay Cool.

Izzie I said, listen, mate, you already make enough money sitting on your devil-worshipping international multi-conglomerate arses. Why don't you think of something really useful to do with it? Like trying to persuade the governments who work for you to stop pumping so many PCBs into the North Sea that the fish'll soon be able to transmit your crappy music just by blowing bubbles? But he put the phone down on me, stupid arse. Hey look, we have a fan in Iran.

Jay You said that?

Izzie I have no idea what I actually said. There are all these things in my head and some of them come out and some of them don't, I can't tell except when people suddenly go all antsy on me and then I reckon they probably came out. Oh, and Maynard rang.

Jay What's he want?

Izzie You know what he wants. He wants to collaborate with you.

Jay No offence, but why would I want to do that?

Izzie He's a great guitarist.

Jay I don't need a guitarist.

Izzie No one wants guitarists any more and he's really really really broke.

Jay Look. I'm sorry he can't get a gig, okay, I empathise. But I'm not a charity.

Izzie Collaboration is not charity, you stupid American.

Jay No, collaboration is what you do if you don't have all the resources. And I don't *need* a guitarist. I have what I need, thank you, and I do not feel the lack of an acoustic dimension right now.

Izzie Hep does.

Jay What?

Izzie On 'All Things Bright and Beautiful'. He feels the lack of an acoustic dimension. That's what he said.

Jay He said that?

Izzie More or less.

Jay Well, okay, if he doesn't want to play it, we'll take it somewhere else.

Izzie No, he likes it –

Jay He's only being asked to *play* it for Chrissakes, no one's asking for an opinion. You see, this is what happens, as soon as you get the middle-men involved, you get this bullshit.

Izzie Jay, it's not bullshit. And he's not a middle man. He is *the* DJ.

Jay I told you we should just stick to the Net.

Izzie Look. The Net's fine, but we need to get a single out. We're not making money from the Net.

Jay Hang on hang on hang on. I never wanted to make money. I just want to make music and suddenly we're having to bend over backwards and kiss the ass of bureaucracy because you want to make money. If people like it they listen to it. They send a bit of money; we're covered. The fans are happy; we're happy. That's democracy. Simple.

Izzie That's not democracy, it's populism. Anyway, Soren doesn't like it.

Jay Who's Soren?

Izzie A fan from Jutland.

Jay A fan? From Jutland? Well what the fuck does he know?

Silence.

Izzie And your mum rang.

Pause.

Jay How did she know I was here?

Izzie She didn't. In fact she told me you were in Thailand this morning.

Jay So why was she calling?

Izzie Were you in Thailand this morning?

Jay Did she think I was here?

Izzie Why would she? She thinks we hate each other.

Jay No, sure, that's right.

Izzie Well, it's not, is it? It's totally bloody wrong, innit? (*Pause.*) Are you ashamed of me?

Jay Of course not. I just don't want to talk to them.

Izzie I think you've established that you can stand on your own two feet now, Jay.

Jay And when was the last time you called yours?

Izzie Oh that's different. They'd be the last people to notice if I went missing.

Jay Exactly. You wouldn't understand.

Izzie No. All parents are the same. They think we should aspire to be more adult, like them. While all they want is to be young, like us.

Jay You have no idea how proprietorial they can be.

Izzie Oh yes I have.

Jay How?

Silence. She looks at him and strokes his face tenderly. He kisses her forehead.

Izzie And you promise me you're not gay?

Jay I'm not gay.

Izzie I've got nothing against it in principle, you know, it's just I'd rather know now than when I'm thirty-five and turkey-basting.

Jay I am not gay.

Izzie You're just happy.

Jay I'm real happy. (*Pause.*) What are you?

Izzie I'm bloody starving, that's what I am.

Jay Then let's go eat. I figure if there's something in your mouth nothing can come out. At least for twenty minutes.

Izzie Then what?

Jay I'm sure I'll think of something.

SCENE FOUR

The grounds of a stately home; Charlotte, Martin, Ed and Lori are having a picnic. Ed is studying a statue of a naked woman which stands nearby.

Lori So let me get this right. If I was the Duke of Norfolk, say, my son would be the Earl and my daughter would be . . . what's a female earl? Early? / Earless?

Martin No. Listen.

Ed (*to Charlotte*) Whaddya reckon?

Martin If you were the Duke then your heir would be a marquess.

Charlotte Lovely.

Ed No, there's definitely a family resemblance.

Charlotte / Oh please.

Lori So which is higher? Duke or earl? Earl or marquess?

Ed Must be the nose.

Martin It goes duke, then marquess, then earl.

Lori So Earl's right at the bottom?

Martin No.

Ed Or maybe the neck?

Martin Then you have viscounts and barons. That's the pecking order. But earl is the oldest rank.

Ed I don't know, beats me.

Lori Can a baron become a duke?

Martin No.

Charlotte But a baroness can become a duchess.

Lori By / marriage, right?

Martin By marriage, yeah. But whether a baron marries higher or lower he retains his hereditary title. It makes no difference.

Lori But he can't marry lower. He's at the bottom.

Charlotte He can marry a commoner.

Martin We're not talking about them.

Charlotte Us. You mean. Us.

Lori So what's a knight?

Martin Oh, that's just a title you get by merit. But if Lady Cavendish, the heir presumptive of the Duke of Devonshire, say, marries Viscount Bradhurst of Little . . . hampton then she goes down two places.

Lori And becomes Viscountess Littlehampton.

Martin No, Viscountess would be her title, but you'd address her as Lady Bradhurst. Littlehampton's just his seat.

Lori Where they live.

Martin No, that's got nothing to do with it. Lord Howland is the son of the Marquess of Tavistock who's the son and heir of the Duke of Bedford and he lives in Switzerland.

Lori But how can someone who is something from somewhere have a son who comes from somewhere else?

Martin Well, that's like saying why doesn't the Duke of Devonshire live in Devon?

Lori Right. (*Pause.*) Why doesn't he?

Martin Oh, for God's sake.

Charlotte Martin!

Martin I'm sorry.

Charlotte Look, nobody puts any store by this sort of thing any more. It's all completely irrelevant. Scotch egg? Or just boiled?

Ed Don't tell me. It was conceived in Wales, bred in Ireland but its grandparents were Scottish. No, thank you. Just boiled.

Lori No, I get a little intense when I'm overexcited. And then my brain freezes up. You think they still live in the house?

Charlotte No.

Lori Her descendants.

Martin So this woman, Marion –

Lori Harriet. She would have been Charlotte's second cousin twice removed. The great-great-granddaughter of Celia Gardner. Here. (*The photo is in her lap. She studies it.*) Don't they look serious?

Ed Why is it that, at the height of their powers, the entire country looks like it just buried its mother?

Lori No, you never see them smile, do you? Oh, of course, bad teeth.

Charlotte No. Showing your teeth was considered a sign of idiocy.

    Pause.

Lori Oh my God.

Ed What is it?

Lori There, look, over there.

Ed Where?

Lori He's coming out.

Ed Oh, Lori.

Lori No, look, he's just standing there.

Ed Lori, you have to stop this. / She keeps imagining –

Lori No, it's one of them, look, stop it, sssh, I'm not talking about –

Ed – she sees Jay. He is not there, Lori. Jay is not there.

Lori – him. Ed, will you just look, there.

Charlotte What?

Lori A man just came out of the house. Over there, look. By the rhododendrons.

Ed Oh, okay.

Lori He just came out into the garden. He's all alone. No, he's talking to someone. It's a child. He's stroking its hair and talking to it. No, it's a dog. Would he be an aristocrat?

Charlotte Sounds like it.

Lori We should go find out.

Martin No, you can't do that.

Charlotte It's private.

Lori Oh, but he might know something.

Martin It's private, Lori. It's a stately home. You can't just go and talk to them.

Pause.

Ed Don't worry about it, honey. You can find what you want in the parish records. (*Silence.*) So if you have one of these titles, what exactly do you pass on?

Charlotte Enormous debt and a very bad dress sense.

Martin That's not true. Max wears nothing but Paul Smith.

Charlotte Yes, but he's gay.

Ed What is this? Cocaine?

Charlotte Salt. You dip your egg in it. We have this friend who's a lord. But he's a lovely man. Nobody knows he's a lord. He's dropped the hyphenated bit from his name and he's just got on with it.

Ed Is he ashamed of being a lord?

Charlotte / Well –

Martin No, he just doesn't want people to think that he thinks he's better than them.

Ed But according to what Charlotte says, they don't.

Martin No. But he doesn't know that.

Charlotte Actually they do.

Martin They don't.

Charlotte No, they do, Martin.

Martin Of course they don't.

Charlotte No, secretly, Martin, they do.

Ed 'They?' Who's they?

Lori The working classes?

Charlotte No.

Martin The working class doesn't exist any more.

Lori Right.

Martin No, the working class is now middle-class.

Ed And the middle class?

Martin And the middle class is now –

Ed Upper-class?

Charlotte Really annoyed.

Ed And the upper class?

Martin Is finished.

Ed So everybody's middle-class?

Martin That's right. We're all equal now. We're *all* middle-class. Except, according to the latest official definition of the term, for us, apparently, because we haven't changed our car in six years, we don't belong to a gym, we haven't been on holiday for two years, never mind her first-class degree from Cambridge or the fact that my grandfather was Second Admiral of the Fleet. Oh no, Izzie, in fact, is the most middle-class of us all because she has earning *potential* conferred on her by her student status and a trendy flat in Notting bloody Hill while we can't afford a pint of sodding milk.

Silence.

Charlotte We're going to have to sell the house.

Lori No! But that's terrible.

Ed Oh, that's too bad.

Lori That's awful. It's such a beautiful house.

Ed I'm very sorry to hear that, Martin. How much is it worth?

Martin Ha! You want to buy it?

Ed No, I –

Martin Only joking.

Ed Couldn't you use it as collateral?

Martin No.

Pause. Charlotte puts her hand out. It's started to rain.

Charlotte Raining again. Sorry. (*She starts packing away the picnic.*)

Ed However, since you don't like the countryside, I guess it could be a relief.

Martin I love the countryside.

Ed I thought you said –

Martin I love the bloody countryside. My family have been here for three hundred years. I love my garden. I love my house. I love my apple trees. It's just the people.

Charlotte Martin, you are the people. He's such a snob.

Martin No, stop it, Charlotte, you don't understand. You have no sense of history.

Charlotte I beg your pardon?

Martin You have no idea – you don't come from *anywhere* or *anyone*, you're adopted, so it doesn't mean anything to you, but my great-great-great-great-grandfather was the original owner of that house, my entire family are buried in the orchard and I have to just hand it over to some rich bastard who'll probably build over the graveyard with a patio and stick a fucking water feature on top of it.

Silence.

Lori You're adopted?

Charlotte Yes.

Lori Oh. (*Silence.*) So . . . Gardner's not your real name?

Charlotte Well. It's the only name I've ever had.

Lori I mean –

Charlotte I know what you mean. (*Pause.*) Yes, I'm adopted. But I don't think of them that way. You see, unless people really know you, they make assumptions, you see, once they know you're adopted. It's just – it's just not something I like to talk about, really.

    Pause.

Ed Sure.

Charlotte They think, oh, that explains it, you know. Me.

Ed Right. / It becomes an issue.

Charlotte As if it makes any difference. Yes, exactly. Until I really get to know someone. It just gets in the way.

    Pause.

Lori But . . .

    Pause. It's raining hard now.

Martin This isn't going to pass.

Charlotte What?

Martin We should go inside.

Charlotte Okay, let's go to the car.

Martin No, we can go in here, look.

Charlotte But we don't want a drink.

Martin Doesn't matter. It's just a café. We can still take shelter.

*They collect everything up and make for the café in
front of them. All, except for Lori, who wanders in
the direction of the car, then stops in the middle of the
lawn, frozen in thought.*

Ed Lori! Hey, Lori!

Charlotte (*to Martin, under her breath*) Thanks, Martin.

Martin I'm sorry.

Ed She doing? (*shouting to Lori*) / We can go in the
café!

Charlotte Jesus. You are such an arsehole sometimes.

Martin I didn't mean to. It just came out.

Ed / Lori! Here, we can go in here!

Martin I'm sorry.

Ed Hey! Over here! Oh, God.

*Ed runs over to Lori and tries to remonstrate with
her, but she firmly pushes him away and remains
where she is, frozen in thought.*

Charlotte Stop saying sorry. Stop apologising and saying
things you don't mean and just do something *right*, will
you, for God's sake, *just try and do something right*.

Martin Like what? Like fawn all over you? Like tell you
what a smart, beautiful, forgiving woman you are? Is that,
would that be *right*?

Pause. Charlotte stares at him.

Charlotte Martin?

Ed returns.

Ed Oh, she's gone crazy, let's get in this café.

They make for the café, but the door is closed in their faces.

Hey. What happened?

Pause.

Martin Excuse me? Excuse me?!

Charlotte He just shut the door in our faces.

Martin OY!

Ed There must be some mistake.

Martin Will you please open the door!

Charlotte He's pretending he can't hear us, look.

Ed Maybe the glass is thick.

Martin Will you please – HELLO? WILL YOU PLEASE OPEN THE DOOR!

Charlotte Maybe he *is* deaf. Maybe he doesn't speak English.

Martin He is, he's foreign. He's not even English. He's Filipino or something.

Charlotte Excuse me! Excuse me! Oh, I'm sorry, this is terrible.

Ed Hey, it's not your fault. Here. (*He tries to shelter her head with his coat.*)

Charlotte No, thanks, I'm all right.

Ed No, come on.

Charlotte I've got a hood.

Ed This is better. Here.

Charlotte Ed. Stop it. Please. Put it on your own head.

Martin He's pretending – can you believe / he's just pretending we're not here.

Charlotte Oh no. Martin. Look. They're closed.

Martin What?

Charlotte It says here they close at four-thirty.

Martin Well it's not four-thirty. It's four twenty-five.

Charlotte Tell him we don't need coffee even. We just need a bit of shelter from the rain.

Martin (*to the waiter*) LOOK. THE BIG HAND IS NOT ON THE SIX!

Ed What the hell kind of a time is four-thirty, anyway?

Martin It's a totally ridiculous, completely fucking stupid time. If he doesn't open the door I'm going to kill him.

Charlotte It's because it's Monday. Of course. Early closing.

Ed Why?

Charlotte Because yesterday was Sunday.

Martin OPEN THE FUCKING DOOR YOU WANKER!

Charlotte Martin, Martin, / it's not worth it.

Martin He's coming over. He's written something on his pad.

Charlotte Oh, he's just a child, look.

Martin He's written something on his pad.

Charlotte What does it say?

   Pause. They all strain their eyes to read.

Martin Piss. Off. We. Closed.

Charlotte Oh.

Pause.

Martin Right. That's it. (*He prepares to charge the door.*)

Charlotte What are you doing? Martin?

Ed I have never encountered such gratuitous incivility in my entire life.

Martin tries to barge the door, but Charlotte gets in the way.

Charlotte I think maybe we should just walk away. Just walk away. Come on. / Ow.

Martin Jesus.

Charlotte Martin, the boy is obviously insane.

Ed (*to Charlotte*) Are you all right? (*to Martin*) This is not the way to handle it. / Where did that man go?

Charlotte Martin, leave it. What man?

Ed I am going to register a formal complaint with his boss.

Charlotte No, you can't do that, Ed.

Ed Why not?

Charlotte You can't just go in their house. They have staff. And dogs. And it's not their fault.

Ed It's not blame I'm looking for. It's responsibility. (*He strides off in the direction in which the aristocrat was sighted.*)

Charlotte Ed! Don't. It's nothing to do with them.

Martin scribbles something on a piece of paper.

No, you can't say that, darling. You're being provocative now.

Martin I am not being provocative. I am defending us all from an ignorant fucking foreigner who can't even write.

Martin holds up his piece of paper. Pause. Charlotte tries to wrest it from him.

Or read.

They struggle over the piece of paper. Until Martin caves in and collapses into her arms.

Charlotte Sssh, come on, Martin, it's okay, it's okay.

SCENE FIVE

Split scene. The sound of rain turns into a drum loop.

Ed and Lori, driving.

Jay's studio: Jay, Maynard and Izzie. Together, Maynard and Jay are creating a mix from a classical track, electronica and guitar. (The technical wording in this will depend on the music composed in rehearsal and will need to be modified accordingly.) Izzie looks on. Jay listens attentively to Maynard while he plays over the sample Jay plays. After a while:

Jay Go to B-minor seventh.

Maynard makes an adjustment; Jay does the same.

Okay, yeah, good. Why don't you do a ripple?

He does.

Keep rippling. (*Jay brings in a new drum loop over the sample.*) Great. Repeat that.

Maynard improvises around the new drum loop.

Too slow. More funky.

Maynard adjusts, but the beat is too dominating for it to make a real difference.

How about – (*He introduces some reverb.*)

Jay No, crap. Start again.

Izzie I like the bit where you went doo-di-doo-di-da-da.

They ignore her and start again. Some way in:

Maynard How about I go back to the dominant? You fill in the beats.

He does and it immediately acquires more energy. Maynard tries something different this time.

Jay Yeah yeah yeah. Just improvise a lead break over this. (*Jay plays off Maynard's improvisation.*) We need some vocals. Not sure what yet.

The music begins to cohere.

Maynard Why don't you take out the cymbal and put in a cowbell on the offbeat.

Jay experiments with various sounds until he finds the right one. They play on . . .

. . . and under Ed and Lori, driving:

Lori Imagine you don't know me. Okay? Pretend you never met me before and you look at me, right? Tell me. Do I look stupid?

Ed I'm driving, Lori, I can't look at you.

Lori You *know* what I look like. I'm saying, imagine you don't know what I look like. Do I look like an idiot?

Ed I think you're taking this the wrong way.

Lori I have been making connections with someone to whom I in fact have no connection. With someone who is pretending to be *related* to me. Is that even her adopted name? Did she make the whole thing up? I mean, what the hell is going on here?

Ed Honey, I don't know why she didn't tell you straight up, but she's a very private person. And they're going through a hard time right now. We have to remember that.

Lori *They're* going through a hard time! What about us?

Ed What about us?

Lori Our son is practically on the disappeared list. We don't even know if he's alive and as far as he is concerned we may as well be dead. I'm trying to distract myself, to take an interest in the past, in my history, which I think I'm doing extremely well, by the way, and suddenly I find that I am part of some large and meaningless joke.

Ed Oh come on, honey. No one's laughing at you.

Lori Well, what the hell are they doing with me?

Ed I don't know. But Martin has revealed himself to have a terrible temper.

Lori I don't blame him. Being shut out in the rain like that.

Ed Sure. But there are ways of doing things.

Lori And ever since we met these people we have not stopped arguing.

Ed What are you talking about?

Lori You see!

Jay's studio:

Jay Nonononono, start again. Let's bring in the sample clean. Let's introduce the acoustics before we bring in the studio sound, yeah?

Maynard Cool.

Izzie What about if it went m-m-m-m-mmm-m and then you came in like you did after the trumpet or whatever it is?

They ignore her again. It is as if she hasn't spoken.

Maynard You want me to suggest the theme or just give you the chord sequence?

Jay Theme, yeah, go for the theme.

Izzie I'll just go and do a bit of housekeeping then, shall I?

Maynard plays. Jay joins in. They improvise together towards a triumphant close, both flushed and elated.

Jay Whadd'ya reckon, Izzie? Good? (*realising the pun*) Or Izzie bad?

Maynard (*picking up the pun and running with it*) Izzie happy? Izzie sad?

Jay Izzie *mad*?

Jay starts improvising on drums, Maynard on guitar.

Maynard Izzie fast? Izzie slow?

Jay Izzie come. Izzie go.

Maynard Izzie gonna stay? Izzie gonna go away?

Izzie goes off in a huff.

Hey hey hey! (*Maynard looks at Jay, bewildered.*) Is she okay?

Jay Fantastic.

Maynard What?

Jay Hey hey hey. Do that again.

Maynard Hey hey hey!

Jay That's it. 'Izzie come, Izzie go.' Let's lay that down. (*He searches through the drum loops for the right place.*)

Ed and Lori, driving:

Lori 'Unless I really know someone.' Jesus. She knows me. I know her. Is there an exam I should take? We're friends, for God's sake.

Ed Damn. I think we just missed the turn.

Lori What turn?

Ed In fact I don't recognise any of this.

Lori Oh my God, and now we're lost.

Ed Was it a left or a right after the sewage farm?

Lori I have no idea.

Ed reverses fast.

You can't do that on a windy lane.

Ed I can do what I like.

Lori Was that it?

Ed It was by a tree.

Lori What kind of tree?

Ed Big. Bushy.

Lori We're in the countryside, Ed. We're surrounded by trees.

Ed Lori, you have to calm down now.

Lori We're lost.

Ed We're not lost. We just don't know where we are.

Lori We're in the middle of the English countryside, miles away from civilisation. It's dark. And we're totally without any reference point to anywhere or anything or anyone.

Ed Just calm down. I'll get us out of this.

Lori Get us out, Ed, get us out of here.

Ed It's okay.

Lori Get us out of this godforsaken country.

SCENE SIX

New York. A fancy restaurant; Ed, Lori, Charlotte, Martin and Timothy sit round a table, having finished eating.

Timothy His lawnmower's broken, right, so he goes next door in the hope of borrowing his neighbour's. Knocks on the door and, as he's standing there, waiting for the guy to open up, he starts thinking of all the objections the neighbour might raise, like, 'I'm sorry but the last time I lent out my lawnmower it came back broken,' or 'I'm afraid it's brand new,' or 'It's too big for your garden,' and so this guy, he works himself up into such a frenzy of indignation over all these imagined excuses, so when his neighbour finally opens the door he shouts at the guy, 'You can keep your goddamn mower, arsehole!'

They laugh.

Ed I love it. / No, I can't compete with that. He has one –

Timothy Isn't it great?

Ed – for every subject, Timothy.

Martin So, you've known each other a long time, then, you guys?

Ed / Oh years.

Timothy Six months.

Ed Well, we've been working together I guess about six months, that's right, but Timothy's / a very famous architect.

Lori He's a famous architect.

Martin Right.

Ed We were lucky to get him.

Timothy No, come on, it's an honour. For me, it's a privilege.

Charlotte Lori was showing us the designs. It looks wonderful.

Lori Oh, and you should see the model. It's going to be a / beautiful building.

Ed It's going to be one of the largest hostels downtown. Capacity, six hundred and fifty.

Charlotte Gosh. How long will that take?

Ed Oh, this is a long-term project. It'll be a good couple of years before it's up and running.

Martin Six hundred and fifty is a lot of people. Wow. And a lot of money. That must involve a lot of money.

    Pause.

Lori Honey, if we're going to make it to this party we should probably pay up, don't you think?

Ed Okay, let's get the William.

Lori It's here. (*She indicates to Ed the bill, which is already on the table.*) Listen, I'm sure you'll be fine if you guys want to come to the party with us. It's dark. No one's going to notice what you're wearing.

Charlotte No, really, it's all right. Thanks.

The men go for their wallets.

Martin Um. We didn't actually have starters, but Charlotte, obviously, had wine.

Ed No, I'm getting this.

Martin I mean, I did have the odd glass –

Ed Martin. This is mine, okay?

Martin Nononono. Let's split it.

Ed Tell the guy, will you, Charlotte.

Charlotte What?

Ed I've got it covered.

Charlotte No, he just wants – we just want to make a contribution, Ed.

Martin Go on, let me just –

Ed Subject closed. Thank you.

Pause.

Martin Well, actually we are quite, you know, at the moment, things are pretty, well, the monkey's on the table, shall we say, so, yeah, thanks.

Ed You're welcome.

Pause.

Timothy So. How long are you guys over for?

Martin It depends.

Charlotte We should be here a while. It depends on this project. But, I mean, it's a great idea, really clever, so, you know.

Timothy No, it sounds interesting.

Martin Well, it's like so many of these things. You look at something for years and then suddenly you see it from another angle / and it reveals itself to you.

Lori Is it a cab ride. West Seventy-Seven.

Ed That's a shame. I could do with a walk. My stomach – I don't know about anybody else but I reckon my lobster's still alive in there.

Timothy No, that was a delicious meal. Thank you, Ed.

Lori Oh, this is by far the best fish restaurant in town.

Timothy God, no, the food here is just excellent. Don't you love this city? Yesterday we had Moroccan. Any day of the week you can have whatever you want.

Charlotte Oh, we've been completely spoilt. Because, you know, it is actually quite expensive for us. People say it's much cheaper here, but actually the difference between the pound and the dollar is negligible.

Timothy Oh no, well, compared to where I come from it's expensive too. No, there's no doubt about it, New York is not cheap.

Martin Really?

Timothy Oh sure, you think about it. The whole place only exists because of money.

Martin Of course, but –

Timothy It's a chimera. Money only exists because of a general consensus that it exists, right? So New York only exists if you believe in it. I remember, when I first flew into JFK, I remember looking down and thinking, wow, it's a mirage, because from above it looks totally flat, like a piece of jigsaw, any minute's going to be washed away

by a large wave. Fragile. And of course that's exactly what it is. It took an act of faith to build it, it takes faith to keep the whole thing going, and now it takes courage just to walk along the darn sidewalk. Which is why it has this energy, this amazing buzz, and everybody's so friendly because, hey, we *all* come from somewhere else. There's no such thing as an insider or an outsider. Not like back home, which I guess is the same for you guys, too. I mean, I've never been to England, but if it's /
anything like where I'm from –

Martin No, that's right, it's the same. I mean, when I say it's the same, I mean it's not like *here*. Obviously England's very different from Japan. Although I have been to Japan, haven't we? And we did find a lot of things in common, actually, I mean, the space thing, for one. Both islands, similar density of population. Obsession with miniature things, and gardens, like us, you love your gardens, don't you? And tea, of course. And dogs. Small dogs. No, I loved Japan. But I have to say I thought Tokyo was one of the most expensive places I've ever been. I suppose it's different outside the capital. Where exactly are you from?

Timothy Ohio.

Pause.

Martin Right.

Timothy But I was, as they say, 'Made in Korea'. (*Pause.*) No, I've never been to Japan. It sounds interesting.

Ed Timothy was talking about New York, as opposed to the rest of the States.

Martin Sure, of course, yes.

Ed There's a big difference.

Martin Yes. Yes, I know.

Silence.

Ed Where's that darn waiter got to?

Charlotte So Lori, have you had any news from Jay?

Lori Not since Latvia.

Charlotte Oh, I'm sorry.

Ed No, if he doesn't want to be found, we don't want to find him. That's the decision we've reached.

Lori But we know he's out there somewhere. Someone who knows someone who knows someone who knows him said they saw him two months ago in a club in San Francisco.

Lori How's Izzie?

Martin No idea.

Charlotte She's at that age, you know, wants to be left alone. But it's so . . . punitive, what he's done. So hard-hearted. I mean, what's his problem?

Lori His problem is that we are controlling, dominating, impatient and pompous.

Charlotte Well, that's ridiculous. *You're* not.

Lori Oh, and snobbish.

Charlotte But he can't just pretend you're not his parents. He can't just deny your relationship, can he?

Lori No, apparently people do, Charlotte. Apparently people can convince themselves that they aren't related to their natural parents in any way. If you feel they've let you down, you can make yourself a whole new life, and you can persuade yourself of this life. Apparently it is possible to re-invent yourself in such a way. And to believe that nothing came before it. Apparently.

Charlotte No, I don't think so. Not for ever. He won't be able to keep it up. He'll call.

Pause.

Lori Maybe.

Silence.

Ed You mean *I am.*

Charlotte Sorry?

Ed Controlling, dominating, aggressive and pompous.

Charlotte No. No, of course not. That's not what I meant.

Ed What did you mean?

Silence.

Martin Thing is, they think in black and white, don't they? Kids. You know, it's like, when they're born, they come out and they can only see things in black and white, babies, can't they? until – what is it? – six weeks before they can see in colour? But they *think* in black and white for a bloody hell of a lot longer than that. Eighteen years, is it, or twenty-one, or thirty-two? I don't know, before they get to think in full three-dimensional Technicolor. Izzie, certainly, doesn't see me as a fully rounded human being yet. But what can you do? I don't know, I've accepted my role as the family doormat. At least you still try. I gave up having any influence over Izzie years ago. Well, we've all got to wipe our feet somewhere, haven't we? If you know what I mean.

Silence.

Ed Yes. I believe I do. (*He indicates for a waiter across the room to come and collect the bill. Then, addressing Lori and Timothy, he stands.*) Let's go party.

Part of a ruin at the edge of a steep hill. Jay and Izzie arrive, breathless and excited; they climb up and survey the valley below. Izzie takes a deep breath and lets out a heartfelt sigh.

Jay You okay?

Izzie I'm on top of the bloody world.

Jay We allowed up here?

Izzie Course we are. It's just an old ruin.

Jay It's eight hundred years old.

Izzie Exactly. Who cares?

Jay It's beautiful. (*Jay takes in the full panorama.*) It makes you want to go to sleep.

Izzie What?

Jay England.

    Pause.

Izzie Is that good?

Jay If you're tired. Yeah.

Izzie Are you?

Jay Wrecked.

    Pause.

Izzie I think they liked us, Jay.

Jay They loved us.

Izzie I think I like you.

Jay You love me.

Izzie What makes you so sure, you cocky bastard?

Jay Because I love you. (*He draws her to him.*)

Izzie So I'm back in favour, then, am I?

Jay You were never out.

Izzie I was. I was excluded. You and Maynard are like a couple of Siamese twins.

Jay You jealous?

Izzie Course not.

Jay He's just a guy. He's a total genius guitar player. But he's just a guy. (*Pause.*) We're something else.

Izzie We're a 'marriage of raw energy and achingly nostalgic string samples', you and me.

Jay Is that right?

Izzie That's what they said. 'The defiant petulance of "No Candy No Can Do" with its backfiring horns and stuttering jump-started beats evolves into the pure unadulterated optimism of "Funfair for the Common Man". This album is a place where the sun is definitely shining, but the dark woods are never far away.' (*Pause.*) Shall I go on?

Jay No.

Izzie 'Bandit proves that innovative, challenging music can be warm, inclusive music too.' And – this is my favourite: 'His guests bring an acute human element and encourage him to pare back his tracks to the very essence of their drama.' I like that one. (*Pause.*) Am I making you uncomfortable? (*He nods.*) There were some really crap ones too. Let me think. 'Marshall is essentially a studio boffin, and despite the edgy acoustics from the wonderful Mr Grant, his attempt to diversify results in blandness.' D'ya know what I mean?!

Jay An 'acute human element' will do.

Suddenly Izzie leaps apart and breaks the intimacy.

Izzie I nearly forgot! (*She delves in her bag and produces a box of sparklers.*)

Jay What?

Izzie Sparklers.

Jay Oh cool.

Izzie Always carry them in case of celebration.

Jay I love these guys.

Izzie Hang on, I've got some matches somewhere.

Jay Do you remember, right, when you were young?

Izzie Yeah?

Jay How you used to write stuff in the air. Well, my dad, right, used to correct my spelling. I'd go, leave me alone, I'm dyslexic, but he'd make me go through the whole packet till I spelt 'Independence Day' properly.

Izzie Bastard.

Jay I made sure I never did.

Izzie Here we go.

Jay Magic.

They light a sparkler each and watch them burn.

Izzie And do you remember how you used to think you had this twin somewhere in the world, someone who looked like you, thought like you, sounded like you and who would understand you even if you told them to bugger off. Do you remember that?

Jay Sure. Can we light another one?

Izzie This time you have to write something.

Jay But you leave my spelling alone, right?

Izzie Right.

Jay makes to throw the dead sparkler over the edge.
Izzie stops him.

Izzie Hey, don't do that. You'd have some poor sheep's eye out. Hey! (*She suddenly straightens up.*) Look at me.

Jay What?

Izzie Look! I'm standing here at the edge of a cliff looking over. Like a normal person.

Jay Normal?

Izzie No vertigo.

Jay Hey, that's good.

Izzie It's amazing. No vertigo. I'm fine.

Jay You're fantastic.

Izzie I'm cured.

Jay How'd you do that?

Izzie Don't know. Didn't have time to think about what could go wrong.

Jay Another one?

They light one more each and write in the air with them.

Izzie What did you write?

Jay 'I love fireworks.' You?

Pause.

Izzie Not telling you.

Jay Go on.

Izzie No.

Jay Okay. Let's go again. Please.

Izzie Bugger off.

Jay Hey. Come on. All right, okay. I'll do one. You watch.

He writes her name in the air. She watches.

SCENE EIGHT

The Marshalls' apartment. The beginning of this scene is a repeat of the end of the first scene in the play. And continued . . .

Ed What I'm saying here is that, usually, and fundamentally, I don't give a damn where you come from, what you do or how much you're worth. And on that basis, we have always believed we had a special relationship with you guys. That we had a connection. However, since your circumstances have changed (and I regret that they have) it appears to have altered the significance of some of those fundamentals. Now, nobody's making any judgements here, but it's a fact that, as human beings, we are all partly defined by our association with one another. And the truth is, when that association starts to impact badly on one side or the other, it's time to question that association, and I'm afraid we have come to the conclusion, albeit with regret, that we don't want to be your friends any more.

Silence. Then Martin begins to laugh.

Martin I've always said, when people say, ' Oh, Americans have no sense of humour,' I always say, 'No, you should meet our friends Ed and Lori.'

Charlotte Martin.

Ed I'm not saying you can't give us a call now and again. We'd be happy to talk to you on the phone. But we just don't think it's appropriate to continue the relationship any further.

   Silence.

Lori I'm so sorry.

Ed No, there's no doubt about it. We are sorry.

Charlotte But. What – I don't –

Martin You're green.

Charlotte What?

Martin You've gone green.

   Charlotte rushes out of the room into the bathroom.
   Silence.

Ed Would you like another glass?

Martin Let me get this right. Are you saying you don't want to associate with us any more because – what are you saying?

Ed I want you to understand that I am not throwing down a gauntlet. I'm not asking you to defend yourselves. And I don't wish to get involved in itemising our disappointments or grievances. I figure we have two incompatible value systems going on here and we should just leave it at that.

   Lori offers Martin some pistachios. He ignores her.

Martin Jesusbloodyfuckinghell.

   Charlotte returns.

Charlotte I can't. The water in the loo is blue.

Martin stands up suddenly and rushes Charlotte out of the room. Silence.

Ed That didn't go too badly.

Lori Oh, I feel terrible.

Ed I thought, there are two ways this could go. One is with dignity. The other is not.

Lori They haven't gone yet

Ed They've gone. Don't worry. They've gone.

Lori You think they'll call?

Ed Why would they do that?

Pause.

Lori No, right, I guess not.

Silence. Martin and Charlotte return. He crosses straight to the picture hanging on the wall and takes it off. Ed jumps up.

Oh.

Ed Hey, no, don't do that.

Lori Martin.

Ed Don't be like that, Martin. Please. Let's not be petty about this.

Lori What are you doing?

Ed Hey, come on. No. That's ours.

Martin It's mine.

Ed It is not yours.

Lori It was a gift.

Ed Put the picture back, Martin. It's not yours.

Martin It bloody is.

Ed No, Martin. It's ours.

Martin It is *my* picture.

Ed If you want to argue about this, we'll pay you for it.

Martin Sorry, mate, but money can't buy you love. Let go.

Ed How much do you want?

Martin Jesus. You think you can just go around *buying* everything. Just *buying* things and selling things and eating things and throwing things away. You think it's all *things*. We are not *things*. We're people. You can't just *sell* us.

Ed Look. You're taking this very personally. We're simply acknowledging that, during the course of our friendship, certain differences have emerged which are unsustainable. The relationship can no longer sustain those differences. Now give me the picture. We like the picture.

Martin No.

Charlotte Let them have it, Martin. I never liked the fucking thing anyway. Come on. I have to get out of here.

Lori You said you loved it.

Ed This is what I mean, Lori, this is what I've been talking to you about.

Martin Give it back.

Ed Oh, this is juvenile. Martin, will you just let go?

Martin Okay.

Martin pulls the picture out of Ed's hands and lets it drop to the floor and smash. Silence.

Charlotte I'm going to be sick.

Charlotte looks for a place to be sick.

Lori That's a terrible thing to do. You're terrible people. You don't care about anything, do you? Don't you care about anything?

Ed Get out.

Martin Yeah, it's been nice knowing you too, you self-satisfied bastard.

Ed Get out. Arsehole.

Martin (*to Charlotte*) I told you he has a temper.

Lori That's just vandalism.

Ed Will you get the hell out of here? Get your ugly sneering face out of my apartment and go back to your whingeing little country with your contempt and your sniping and your misery and your failure and your pessimism and go piss on your own bonfire.

Silence.

Martin Just what exactly makes you think you're better than us?

Charlotte lights on the bowl of pistachios. She empties it onto the table and vomits into it.

Ed I don't think we're better than you. We *are* better than you. We're honest. We don't go round making things up and mocking people and pretending to be people we're not.

Pause.

Martin Oh, that.

Ed We may be overbearing and aggressive and whatever else but we do not invent the truth.

Martin All right, so Charlotte's adopted –

Ed No, actually, it is not all right. Charlotte is not a Gardner. You are not in any way related, but you have, out of some twisted notion of privacy, you have encouraged my wife into making connections with you which are spurious and unfounded and which make her look like a complete and total idiot. Gardner is not your name.

Charlotte It's the only name I have.

Ed It is not who you are.

Charlotte Oh, right. Well, who the fuck am I, then?

Ed I couldn't have put it better myself.

Charlotte You presume to know me because of my name and now you think you *don't* know me because it's not. Well, if the only reason you befriended us was because of my name then you're the bloody arsehole.

Ed That is not what I'm saying –

Martin Well what are you saying, because / quite honestly –

Ed Will you shut up, you goddamn idiot son of a bitch? I'm saying. You're disingenuous liars.

  Silence.

Martin What I can't stand, you see, what I can't stand is the way you Americans have to simplify everything.

Lori I don't understand. Were you laughing at us all the time? / We just don't understand.

Charlotte No, you don't understand. That's the point. If I thought you understood, I would have told you earlier. A lot of people know I'm adopted, it's not a secret.

Lori But there's nothing wrong with being adopted.

Charlotte *I know there's nothing wrong with being adopted.* But I'm not going to reveal my inner self to someone who for the first time in their entire life has only just realised that beyond the fluffy pink insulated walls of their tiny world people actually get old, get ill, and *die.*

Lori I don't understand.

Martin Look. We didn't ask you to befriend us. We didn't ask you to throw your money down our toilet and dole out patronage like a couple of Victorian imperialists, prancing round the English countryside looking for evidence of your genetic superioriy. *You* befriended *us.* And now you've discovered we're not good enough or rich enough or successful enough for you and you think you can just dump us. Well, let me tell you something. We don't care.

Ed Indifference is hardly a point of pride.

Martin We don't care because *we know who we are.*

Pause.

Lori Who?

Martin You're just *children*, aren't you? You haven't a clue. You think the world centres around you and the toys in your bloody cot. Well, we're English. We have history. We have complex philosophies. And we have nothing to prove.

Ed Well, maybe that's your problem. You sit there with your class system up your ass just waiting for a handout. You have no principles, you have nothing but your pathetic past to be proud of.

Martin I don't know what you're talking about. I don't believe I've ever asked anyone for a handout.

Ed You don't *believe* in anything.

Martin Oh what, like *democracy*, you mean? Or *regime change*? Or like *Operation World Fucking Domination*, you mean? / You don't get it, do you? You think you –

Ed No that is not what I mean.

Martin – have an answer for everything. You think it's all about solutions. Well, let me tell you something. It's not about providing *answers*. It's about asking *questions*.

Ed Okay. I have a question for you.

Martin What?

Ed Why is your wife wiping her hands on my cushions?

Charlotte I'm not.

Ed I saw you.

Martin Fuck your cushions. Don't try and change the subject.

Ed You lie and you despoil everything. I'm not changing the subject. That's what you do. You stand there, on your dirty little island, spewing bile on everyone who isn't like you. / Bitching to us about Europe, then bitching to Europe about –

Charlotte It's better than dropping bombs on everyone who isn't like you.

Ed – us. I beg your pardon?

Charlotte It's better than dropping bombs on weddings and marketplaces or shooting children and grannies and people who are on the same bloody side as you.

Ed Oh Jesus.

Charlotte Or tearing up treaties which might involve you in having to subject your criminals or your cars and your fridges to the same laws as the rest of us.

Ed As a matter of fact / we invented environmentalism.

Charlotte The rest of us have rules, structures, systems. Bollocks you did. Not an arbitrary set of self-regulating, self-serving made-up laws that allow rich people to get away with murder while everyone else has to watch them on television. Our government is responsible to its people. Our judicial system is subject to law. And our accountants, believe it or not, are accountable.

Ed Don't you talk to me about laws and systems with your highest crime rate in Europe and your collapsing infrastructure and your rude, incompetent, *ugly* people and your arse-licking prime minister. It's pathetic. One minute you're in trouble, you shout help, we come running, next minute, we have to listen to your horseshit lectures on how to run our goddamn country. You can't even run your own country. You have a Scotsman in charge, you get an American to fix your Underground, a Swede to manage your soccer team while all you do is jerk around forming committees and sub-committees with regard to the content of your own diapers. You're nothing but a bunch of hypocritical half-arsed peasants.

Martin At least we have *society*. Your country is held together by nothing but a whining ego. And at least we elected our arse-licking prime minister. Our country is run by its democratically elected representatives. Not some illiterate trigger-happy ex-alcoholic who can barely speak English.

Ed He has nothing to do with me.

Martin He has everything to do with you. He's an American. He couldn't be anything else. He's corrupt, strident and ignorant. And licking arse is better than kicking it.

Ed Well that says more about you than I care to know.

Martin Oh shut up, you fucking twat.

Lori Oh God, this is so awful. Can we start again?

Ed / No!

Martin No!

Ed I am beginning to realise how seriously I underestimated the depth of your contempt, but I remain totally mystified by your assumption of superiority. You are small, you are mean and (*as he passes Charlotte*) yes, you smell of sick.

Lori bursts into tears.

Lori It wasn't meant to be like this . . . we're not like that . . . you can't say things . . . you can't . . . it's all wrong . . . we trusted you . . . it's all about trust, isn't it? . . . and you just –

Martin Trust as in what sense of the word? As in split capital investment trust?

Lori The point is, we liked you . . . and suddenly we find . . . out of the blue . . . this is what you think of us . . . I introduced you to all my friends . . . and all along, you have deceived us into thinking we were friends, and all along you hated us.

Martin How dare you – you're the ones who are chucking us. How dare you cry?

Lori Stop it, please stop it now.

Martin You started it, for fuck's sake. It's not out of the blue, is it? You started it. Like September 11th. The collapse of the stock market. The project for the new American fucking century. You bloody started it.

Lori What are you talking about?

Martin *Consequences.* I'm talking about *consequences.*

Ed Oh. And from what particular pedestal are you talking about these consequences?

Martin Jesus, and you're surprised Jay left home? Poor guy had to put up with your neurotic, liberal bullying fascism all those years. It's no wonder he's retarded.

Ed suddenly punches Martin squarely in the face. He is temporarily stunned, then tries to return the punch, but Charlotte stops him.

Charlotte No, Martin, don't, don't, it's not worth it.

Silence.

Ed There's nothing more I have to say. All we are asking for now is closure.

Martin Closure?

Ed Closure.

Silence. Then Charlotte starts to laugh.

Charlotte I distinctly remember the day I woke up and my face had sat down. I looked in the mirror and it was like my face had just sat down. Overnight. And I remember thinking, it's the end of the world. (*Pause.*) Closure, my arse. Who the hell do you think you are? (*Charlotte is breathing erratically; it looks like she might be sick again.*)

Martin Charlotte. Are you okay?

Charlotte (*she gathers herself up briskly*) Much better, thanks. Are you?

He nods.

Can we go now?

Martin Come on.

He puts his arm around her and they leave. Silence.

Lori They don't care. About anything.

Ed Are you okay?

Lori shakes her head.

It's okay, honey. It's over. It's okay now. It's okay.

SCENE NINE

Izzie's flat. Izzie and Jay. Jay toys with a phone in his hand.

Izzie What are they gonna say?

Jay It's cool.

Izzie I know it's cool, but what are they gonna say?

Jay She'll cry and he'll say, 'So when are you getting married?'

Izzie When are we getting married?

Jay Whenever you like.

Izzie After it's born. Not before. I don't want people to think that's w*hy* we're getting married.

Jay People can say what they damn well like. It's not why we're getting married.

Izzie Why are we getting married?

Jay Because we're both orphans with no one else to turn to. We have no past. We have only the future. And because you taste like blueberry muffins.

Izzie Where are we going to live?

Jay Let's toss.

Izzie What?

Jay Heads, here – tails, there.

Izzie Heads.

He does.

Oh fuck. No. Do it again.

Jay Hey. It's the luck of the dice.

Izzie No, I want to be in New York.

Jay You don't want to have a baby in New York. You want to have it in green fields surrounded by sheep. What are yours going to say?

Izzie 'I knew it.' Mum's going to say, 'I knew it all along.' (*Izzie flinches.*)

Jay What? Did it move?

Izzie No, you stupid Yank, it's only seven weeks. (*Pause.*) Maybe we should tell them after the scan. They might start interfering and wanting to know what the sex is and what we're going to call it.

Jay We can tell them what the sex is, but names are out.

Izzie She's going to be so chuffed.

Jay They're going to take the credit, though.

Izzie Well, they started it.

Jay I suppose they should take some credit.

Izzie They should.

Pause. Jay begins to dial a number.

I don't want to know what the sex is.

Jay What?

Izzie You said, 'We can tell them what the sex is.' I don't want to know what it is.

Jay Why not? You think it might change?

Izzie You want to know what the sex is?

Jay Course I do.

Izzie Why?

Jay Because the information is there. Are you crazy? Why not?

Izzie But why?

Jay Why not?

Izzie No, why?

Jay Uhuh. Why not?

Izzie No. Why?

Jay Because why not?

Izzie No, the question is *why*?

Jay Uhuh, the question is *why not*?

And in the distance, on the other side of the Atlantic, the phone rings.

The End.